GROWING IN KNOWLEDGE
Living by Faith

GROWING IN KNOWLEDGE
Living by Faith

AN INTERACTIVE HANDBOOK ON BASIC CHRISTIAN TRUTHS

FRANK R. SHIVERS

Frank Shivers Evangelistic Association

Columbia, SC

©2011 by Frank Shivers Evangelistic Association
International Standard Book Number: 187812708X
Published in association with New Vantage Partners—Franklin, TN
info@NewVantagePartners.net
Cover and interior design by Paul Gant Art & Design—Franklin, TN

Unless otherwise noted, Scripture quotations are from
The Holy Bible King James Version

ALL RIGHTS RESERVED
Permission may be granted upon written request for reproducing portions
of this volume.

For information
P.O. Box 9991
Columbia, South Carolina 29290
www.frankshivers.com

Library of Congress Cataloging - in - Publication Data

Shivers, Frank R., 1949 –
Growing in Knowledge, Living by Faith
/ Frank Shivers

Library of Congress Control Number:
2010943450

Printed in the United States of America

Dedicated to those in passionate pursuit to know God intimately, understand His Word thoroughly, obey Him fully, and serve Him faithfully; and to those who have yet to start the journey.

*"Faith proves unseen things,
not for itself only, but for other men.
By your faith you demonstrate the reality
of the unseen to the world at large.
You bring the unseen things into sight
by your faith. By the victory your faith wins
you prove faith and prove the unseen things
to the man of the world. By your strength
in the hour of agony,
I come to believe in God more perfectly."*[1]

—G. Campbell Morgan

GROWING IN KNOWLEDGE, LIVING BY FAITH

CONTENTS

INTRODUCTION...2

UNIT 1—BELIEVE THIS!...6
- Word Wisdom: Sin, Covenant, Atonement, Trinity

UNIT 2—THE NEW BIRTH...22
- Word Wisdom: Born Again, New Birth, Regeneration, Salvation
- Neglect Not: Salvation

UNIT 3—THE SIGNIFICANCE OF THE BIBLE...30
- Word Wisdom: Infallibility, Inerrancy, Prophecy, Inspiration
- Neglect Not: Scripture

UNIT 4—OVERVIEW OF THE BIBLE...40
- Word Wisdom: Grace, Mercy, Faith

UNIT 5—PRAYER, FASTING, AND SOLITUDE...48
- Word Wisdom: Sanctification, Carnal, Holiness
- Neglect Not: Supplication

UNIT 6—BAPTISM...62
- Word Wisdom: Adoption, Confession, Justification, Repentance
- Neglect Not: Daily Dying to Self

UNIT 7—THE LORD'S SUPPER...68
- Word Wisdom: Messiah, Resurrection, Glorification
- Neglect Not: Self-Examination

UNIT 8—STEWARDSHIP...74
- Word Wisdom: Hallelujah, Amen, Temptation
- Neglect Not: Stewardship

UNIT 9—SATAN...86
- Word Wisdom: Demons, Millennium, Armageddon
- Neglect Not: The Second Coming

UNIT 10—WITNESSING...96
- Word Wisdom: Depravity, Eternal Security, Inheritance, Election
- Neglect Not: Soulwinning

UNIT 11—CHURCH...106
- Word Wisdom: Christian, Church, Rapture
- Neglect Not: The Sanctuary

UNIT 12—UNDERSTANDING GOD'S WILL...120
- Word Wisdom: Spiritual Gifts, Hypocrisy, Tribulation
- Neglect Not: Service

ENDNOTES...134

INTRODUCTION

Christian growth is work.

How's that for a hopeful promise with which to start this study? Paul emphasizes in Philippians 2:12: "*Work* out your own salvation with fear and trembling (italics mine)."

The words "work out" are used by the first century author Strabo to refer to digging silver out of mines, a task requiring diligent and exhausting labor. Similarly, Christians are to dig out of their salvation its fullest blessings, beliefs, and benefits. But the rewards are well worth the effort:

> Let your roots grow down into him, and let your lives be built on him.
> Then your faith will grow strong in the truth you were taught, and you
> will overflow with thankfulness. (Colossians 2:7, NLT)

Peter continues the theme by saying we are to "add to your faith virtue"—or as another translation renders, "Furnish your faith with resolution" (2 Peter 1:5). Oswald Chambers explains this verse:

> "Add" means to get in the habit of doing things, and in the initial stages it
> is difficult. To take the initiative is to make a beginning, to instruct your-
> self in the way you have to go.[2]

Although you were saved in the twinkling of an eye the moment you confessed Christ as Lord and Savior, it will take months (years?) of heart work to mature in the faith. This heart work *in* you is necessary for God to work *through* you.

PLAN OF ACTION

This study is designed to be your assistant in this work. The first chapter explores foundational Christian beliefs paramount for spiritual growth. Subsequent chapters address subjects like New Birth, the Church, Prayer, Bible Study, Baptism, the Lord's Supper, Stewardship, Satan, Witnessing, and Understanding the Will of God. Throughout, you'll find key Bible words, fascinating and inspiring quotes from saints through the centuries, and the "Neglect Not's" of growth.

Each unit offers the chance to review the material as you go and then reflect for yourself on the deeper meanings to be drawn from the teachings. Finally, you'll be encouraged to respond appropriately to whatever new things God has revealed to you through your study. I encourage you to work through each session prayerfully and thoroughly.

Growing in Knowledge, Living by Faith is designed for pastor classes, Sunday school programs, and camp or retreat curriculum. It also may be distributed to individual new believers or church members for personal study. Since this workbook functions equally well as a personal or group study, there is a fair amount of flexibility in how you can go through it.

GROWING IN KNOWLEDGE, LIVING BY FAITH

If you're using the study with a group, the unit structure can be tailored to the time period during which you plan to complete the study. The optimum approach is to work through one unit each week for twelve weeks. If a lesser period is available—six weeks, for instance—units can be combined as noted below to finish within the shorter timeframe.

SIMMERING IN THE WORD

The Apostle Paul aspired "to know Him [Christ] and the power of His resurrection, and the fellowship of His sufferings, being made conformable unto His death" (Philippians 3:10). He knew

---

RECOMMENDED SCHEDULE FOR 6-WEEK STUDY

WEEK 1—
Units 1 & 10 "This We Believe" and "Witnessing"

WEEK 2—
Units 2 & 6 "New Birth" and "Baptism"

WEEK 3—
Units 3 & 4 "The Significance of the Bible" and "Overview of the Bible"

WEEK 4—
Units 5 & 8 "Prayer, Fasting, and Solitude" and "Stewardship"

WEEK 5—
Units 7 & 9 "The Lord's Supper" and "Satan"

WEEK 6—
Units 11 & 12 "Church" and "Understanding God's Will"

INTRODUCTION

Christ as Savior, but he longed to know Him more intimately. It was Paul's never-ending pursuit. The verb "know" means "to know by experience," demonstrating that Paul would not be content with simple head knowledge or second-hand knowledge of Christ.

Do you share Paul's aspiration? Do you hunger and thirst to know Christ more intimately? Let this be your focus—not just how much sin you can avoid or how much good you can do. Spiritual disciplines simply become legalistic weights if their purpose is not to propel you to know Christ more deeply. Christians must keep the main thing the main thing.

The two ways to make tea illustrate two methods of spiritual growth. The first is to boil water and dip the tea bag in and out of the water until it's ready. The second is to boil water and simply place the tea bag in the water until done. You don't want to be the type of believer who dips in and out of the church, Bible study, prayer, godliness, and fellowship with Christ. Your best growth will occur only when you abide (stay put) in the disciplines without wavering (John 15:4-7).

The London pastor C. H. Spurgeon never tired in his personal work of growing in Christ:

> The longer I live, the more sure do I become that our happiness in life, our comfort in trouble, and our strength for service all depend upon our living near to God, nay, dwelling in God, as the lilies in the water...I would rather spend an hour in the presence of the Lord than a century in prosperity without Him...He who lives without prayer, he who lives with little prayer, he who seldom reads the Word, and he who seldom looks up to heaven for a fresh influence from on high—he will be the man whose heart will become dry and barren. However, he who falls in secret on his God, who spends much time in holy retirement, who delights to meditate on the words of the Most High, and whose soul is given up to Christ—such a man must have an overflowing heart. As his heart is, such will his life be.[3]

Marie Barnett captured the heart of intimacy for Christ that all believers should exhibit:

> And I, I'm desperate for You, And I, I'm lost without You.
> Oh Lord, I'm lost without You. I'm lost without You.
> This is the air I breathe; this is the air I breathe
> Your Holy presence living in me.[4]

> *"A thousand distractions would woo us away from thoughts of God, but if we are wise we will sternly put them from us and make room for the King— and take time to entertain Him! Progress in the Christian life is exactly equal to the growing knowledge we gain of the Triune God in personal experience. And such experience requires a whole life devoted to it and plenty of time at the holy task of cultivating God."[5]*
>
> — A.W. Tozer

It is my prayer these studies will richly bless, instruct and enable your spiritual growth, that you may "...grow in grace, and in the knowledge of our Lord and Savior Jesus Christ. To him be glory both now and forever" (2 Peter 3:18).

(Note: All resources recommended in this book can be purchased at www.frankshivers.com)

UNIT 1

BELIEVE THIS!

Christians must know what they believe and why they believe it so as to "be ready always to give an answer to every man that asketh you a reason of the hope that is in you with meekness and fear" (1 Peter 3:15). With that biblical directive in mind, we begin our study with a simple and concise presentation of core Christian beliefs on which to build a thorough and biblically sound theology. A foundational understanding of biblical theology (doctrinal beliefs) is essential to maturing as a Christian. Doctrinal deficiency results in spiritual illiteracy and stunted growth.

> "My people are destroyed for a lack of knowledge."
>
> (Hosea 4:6)

> "It is a great thing to begin the Christian life by believing good solid doctrine....I thank God that He early taught me the gospel, and I have been so perfectly satisfied with it, that I do not want to know any other."[6]
>
> —C. H. Spurgeon

> "The devil disturbs the church as much by error as by evil. When he cannot entice Christian people into sin, he deceives them with false doctrine."[7]
>
> —John Stott

BELIEVE THIS—*About God*

> "[God] is Himself the great central source and originator of all power."[8]
> —Charles H. Spurgeon

GOD IS OMNIPOTENT.
That means He is all-powerful and can do anything He wants to. No man or nation can stop Him.

GOD IS OMNISCIENT.
He is all-knowing. There is nothing God isn't already aware of. Nothing has ever "occurred" to God. He already knew it.

GOD IS OMNIPRESENT.
He is present everywhere at the same time.

> "Omni-" means all, completely, or universally.

GOD IS IMMUTABLE.
"Immutable" means He never changes. He is always the same as He ever was.

GROWING IN KNOWLEDGE, LIVING BY FAITH

UNIT 1

"Jesus Christ the same yesterday, and today, and forever."
(Hebrews 13:8)

GOD IS LOVE.

God loves man and desires him to be saved. This love of God is uninfluenced by anything man has done or may do and is never ending.

"We love Him because He first loved us."
(1 John 4:19)

GOD IS HOLY AND RIGHTEOUS.

God is incapable of doing wrong and always does what is right (Isaiah 6:3). In His holiness, God cannot tolerate sin. He hates what it does in the person who sins and the impact it has on others and the world He has made.

GOD IS MERCIFUL.

He is always ready to forgive the sinner and seeks to reconcile the wrongdoer to Himself (2 Corinthians 5:18-19; Ephesians 2:4).

GOD IS AUTHOR.

God is the creator, owner, and sustainer of all that exists (Colossians 1:16-17).

REVIEW

(1) What are the eight attributes of God? _____
_____

(2) Where does God's power come from? ___self.

(3) God is love, He is holy, and He is merciful. How do these attributes naturally go together?
_____

(4) "In the beginning, _____ created the _____ and the _____." (Genesis 1:1)

BELIEVE THIS!
UNIT 1

BELIEVE THIS—*About the Trinity*

Christians believe in one God, but this God exists in three Persons. These three share one nature and are God the Father, God the Son, and God the Holy Spirit simultaneously. Christians call this the Trinity. D.L. Moody compared the Trinity to a triangle which is one figure, yet with three different sides at the same time. Patrick of Ireland used a shamrock to explain the Trinity. Holding up a shamrock, he would ask people, "Is it one leaf or three?" To which they would reply, "It is both one leaf and three." "And it is so with God," he would conclude.

"The eternal triune God reveals Himself to us as Father, Son, and Holy Spirit, with distinct personal attributes, but without division of nature, essence, or being."
—The 2002 Baptist Faith and Message

"There is only one 'What' (essence) in God, but there are three 'Whos' (persons) in that one 'What'."[9]
—Norman Geisler

> **WORD WISDOM : TRINITY**
>
> A term used to describe that God is a unity of three Persons: God the Father, God the Son, and God the Holy Spirit (Matthew 28:19).
>
> Although the word "Trinity" does not occur in the Bible, the Trinitarian doctrine is revealed in texts such as *Genesis 1:26; 3:22; Numbers 6:24–26; Isaiah 48: 16; Matthew 28:19; 2 Corinthians 13:14; John 14:25–31; 1 John 5:6–8*. This doctrine is presented in Scripture but not explained. It is authenticated overwhelmingly in the biblical text.

REVIEW

C.H. Spurgeon said:

> How unwisely do those believers talk who make preferences in the Persons of the Trinity; who think of Jesus as if he were the embodiment of everything lovely and gracious, while the Father they regard as severely just, but destitute of kindness. Equally wrong are those who magnify the decree of the Father, and the atonement of the Son, so as to depreciate the work of the Spirit. In deeds of grace, none of the Persons of the Trinity act apart from the rest. They are as united in their deeds as in their essence. In their love towards the chosen they are one, and in the actions which flow from that great central source they are still undivided.[10]

With Spurgeon's advice in mind, briefly explain in your own words what is wrong with thinking of Jesus, the Father, and the Holy Spirit as having different attributes: _____
_____

GROWING IN KNOWLEDGE, LIVING BY FAITH
UNIT 1

BELIEVE THIS—*About the Bible*

There is no other book like the Bible. Christians believe the Bible is God's only written revelation to man. It took 40 different men more than 1500 years to write the Bible's 66 books—39 in the Old Testament (before Christ) and 27 in the New Testament (beginning with the story of Christ).

Totally true in fact and doctrine, the Bible contains no contradictions and is thoroughly trustworthy. "Through the Holy Spirit's agency, God is involved in both the production and interpretation of Scripture. Men of God in antiquity spoke as they were moved by the Holy Spirit. 'Moved' means literally 'to bear along.' Scripture is infallible precisely because the Holy Spirit 'bore along' the prophets who spoke and wrote."[11] See 1 Peter 1:20-21. The Bible is not simply to be believed, but it is to be applied to one's life (James 1:22).

> More copies of the Bible have been printed than any other book in history, according to *Smith's Bible Dictionary*.

"More than 5,000 manuscripts of the New Testament exist today, which makes the New Testament the best-attested document of all ancient writings."[12]

— Charles C. Ryrie

Theologian John Stott explains the relationship of a believer to Scripture:

> The Christian is under both instruction and authority. He looks to Jesus as his Teacher to instruct him, and as his Lord to command him. He believes what he believes because Jesus taught it, and he does what he does because Jesus told him to do it….Our view of Scripture is derived from Christ's view of Scripture, just as our view of discipleship, of heaven and hell, of the Christian life, and of everything else, is derived from Jesus Christ. Any question about the inspiration of Scripture and its authority therefore resolves itself to: "What did Jesus Christ teach about these points?"…To sum up, the authority of Scripture is due to the inspiration of Scripture. The Old and New Testaments are authoritative in our lives, because they are in fact inspired. And therefore, since Jesus Christ is our Teacher as well as our Lord, the authority of Christ and the authority of Scripture stand or fall together.[13]

W.A. Criswell in *Why I Preach that the Bible is Literally True* similarly notes:

> Jesus believed and taught the infallibility of Scripture. He regarded it as divine authority and as the final court of appeal concerning all questions. He sets His seal to its historicity and its revelation from God. He supplements it, but never supplants it. He amplifies it, but He never nullifies it. He modifies it according to His own divine prerogative, He fulfills it according to His divine mission, but He never lessens its divine authority. His attitude towards the Scripture was one of total trust. It was the direct written Word of God to man.[14]

BELIEVE THIS!
UNIT 1

> *"All of this Book I believe. Not some of it, not most of it, not part of it, but ALL of it! Inspired in totality, the Miracle Book of diversity and unity of harmony and infinite complexity."*[15]
>
> —R. G. Lee

In *You Can Trust The Bible*, Stott also offers a creative view of Scripture as God's story about Himself:

> The Bible is God's self-disclosure, the divine autobiography. In the Bible the subject and the object are identical, for in it God is speaking about God. He makes himself known progressively in the rich variety of his being: as the Creator of the universe and of human beings in his own image, the climax of his creation; as the living God who sustains and animates everything he has made; as the covenant God who chose Abraham, Isaac, Jacob and their descendants to be his special people; and as a gracious God who is slow to anger and quick to forgive, but also as a righteous God who punishes idolatry and injustice among his own people as well as in the pagan nations. Then in the New Testament he reveals himself as the Father of our Lord and Savior Jesus Christ, who sent him into the world to take our nature upon him, to be born and grow, live and teach, work and suffer, die and rise, occupy the throne and send the Holy Spirit; next as the God of the new covenant community, the church, who sends his people into the world as his witnesses and his servants in the power of the Holy Spirit; and finally as the God who one day will send Jesus Christ in power and glory to save, to judge and to reign, who will create a new universe, and who in the end will be everything to everybody.[16]

REVIEW

(1) How many errors have been discovered in the Bible? _____
(2) What contradictions have been found in the Bible? _____
(3) The Bible contains historical narratives, poetry, prophetic writings, and letters. Why do you think so many kinds of literature are needed to tell the autobiography of God?

_____
_____
_____
_____
_____
_____

GROWING IN KNOWLEDGE, LIVING BY FAITH
UNIT 1

BELIEVE THIS—*About Sin and Satan*

Sin is failure to keep God's law (Exodus 20) and any act whatsoever that does not glorify God (1 Corinthians 10:31). Disobedience to the will of God (sin), results in separation from God temporarily and eternally. Sin entered the human race in the Garden of Eden when Adam and Eve disobeyed God. Scripture states, "Wherefore, as by one man sin entered into the world, and death by sin; and so death passed upon all men, for that all have sinned" (Romans 5:12). It is now a condition of all men and women: "All have sinned" (Romans 3:23).

> **WORD WISDOM : SIN**
>
> Any violation of the Law of God; acts of defilement and defiance (*1 John 3:4*). All have sinned (*Romans 3:23; 1 John 1:8, 10*). C.H. Spurgeon says, "One sin can ruin a soul for ever; it is not in the power of the human mind to grasp the infinity of evil that slumbereth in the bowels of one solitary sin."[17]

Lucifer was an anointed cherub of God (Ezekiel 28:14) who, because of his extreme pride, rebelled against God. After falling from his high position (Isaiah 14:12), he became known as Satan. He possesses intelligence (2 Corinthians 2:11), memory (Matthew 4:6), a will (2 Timothy 2:26), a desire (Luke 22:31), wrath (Revelation 12:12), and great organizational ability (1 Timothy 4:1; Revelation 2:9, 24). His purpose is to usurp God's authority in the world by deceiving, lying, tempting, and destroying (John 10:10). Unlike God, though, Satan is not omnipresent. He is not everywhere at once but employs countless demons ("unclean spirits," "evil spirits," "deceiving spirits") throughout the earth to antagonize and attack the believer (Matthew 10:1; Acts 19:12-13; 1 Timothy 4:1; Revelation 16:14). But the believer is promised victory over Satan's tactics (1 John 4:4).

Some of Jesus' primary reasons for coming to earth were to overthrow Satan, neutralize his power (Matthew 12:25-29; John 12:31), and cast him and his demons into eternal damnation in the Lake of Fire and Brimstone (Matthew 25:41; Revelation 20:10). Knowing this about Jesus' plan for Satan helps our understanding of hell. God created hell for Satan and his demons, not for mankind. Nevertheless, anyone who lives alienated from God in rebellion and unbelief will suffer this eternal punishment. Yet God longs for all to be saved so that no one experiences the torment of hell.

REVIEW

(1) Which of the following describes sin?
❏ Failure to keep God's law   ❏ Disobedience to God's will   ❏ Any act or thought that does not bring glory to God
(2) The result of sin is _____ from God. For how long? _____
(3) What two people committed the first sins? _____ and _____
(4) _____ rebelled against God and then became known as Satan.
(5) Satan is an impersonal force. True _____ False _____
(6) Name some of the tactics Satan uses against people. _____
_____
(7) For whom did God create hell? _____

BELIEVE THIS!
UNIT 1

BELIEVE THIS—*About Salvation*

In God's salvation covenant with mankind, God loved the world so much that He sent His only son to die upon a cross to make possible the forgiveness of man's sins (John 3:16). Only Jesus' death, burial and resurrection can atone for (forgive) sin. To repent of sin means to express genuine sorrow for rejecting Christ and a change of mind about the role of Christ in your life. When a person repents and exhibits personal trust in Jesus Christ, he or she is saved (Acts 20:21). This salvation is a free gift of God, available to all people. According to the salvation covenant, it cannot be earned, merited, or deserved. It can only be received as a gift of God (Ephesians 2:8-9).

> *"God does not predestine some people to Heaven and others to Hell. God desires that all should be saved. God gives us a will; we can choose to either accept Jesus or reject Him."*[18]
>
> —Adrian Rogers

WORD WISDOM : COVENANT

A binding agreement or contract between God and man. It may be conditional or unconditional. There are eight important covenants in the Bible:
- Salvation covenant with man (*Titus 1:1-2; Hebrews 13:20*);
- Covenant with Adam (*Genesis 1:28; 2:15-17; 3:15-19*);
- Covenant with Noah (*Genesis 8:21-22*);
- Covenant with Abraham (*Genesis 12: 2-3, 7; 13:14-17; 15:5, 18; 17:8*);
- Covenant with Moses and Israel (*Exodus 19: 3-8; Leviticus 26; Deuteronomy 28*);
- Covenant with David (*2 Chronicles 13:5; 2 Samuel 7:12-16;23:5*);
- Covenant with the Church (*Matthew 16:18; 26:28; Luke 22:20; Hebrews 13:20-21*);
- New Covenant with Israel
  (*Jeremiah 31:31-34; Isaiah 42:6; Isaiah 43:1-6; Deuteronomy 1:1-9; Hebrews 8:7-12*).

REVIEW

(1) What was God's "price" of entering the salvation covenant with mankind? _____

(2) What is the "price" of a person's entry into the salvation covenant with God? _____

(3) To whom is the salvation covenant available? _____

GROWING IN KNOWLEDGE, LIVING BY FAITH

UNIT 1

BELIEVE THIS—*About Eternal Security*

A person "born again" into the family of God can never be "unborn" (John 5:24). Jesus' promise of abundant and eternal life to all who repent and believe is certain (John 10:10; Acts 20:21) and trustworthy. Satan may attack and assault the believers' faith, but he can never steal it. He can never undo what God has done in salvation. At the moment of salvation, the believer's name is written with permanent ink in the Lamb's Book of Life and neither Satan, demons, nor man can erase it (Romans 8:31-39).

> *"No one can steal the Christian's treasure, and no one can disqualify him from receiving it."*[19]
>
> —John MacArthur

WORD WISDOM : ATONEMENT

At-one-ment, the state of being reconciled to God by means of Jesus' death, burial and resurrection (*Romans 5:11*). Man in his inherent state is alienated from God by sin (*Colossians 1:21; Ephesians 2:12*). Jesus Christ bridges the chasm of separation for all who receive Him as Lord and Savior making them right with God (*1 Timothy 2:5*).

Jesus teaches in John 6:37 that all who come to Him in repentance and faith are saved and that they are saved permanently. No one can "lose" his or her salvation. In John 6:39-40, Jesus says He will not lose anyone who is added to the Kingdom by New Birth. The Apostle Peter declares that the Christian is "kept by the power of God" unto salvation (1 Peter 1:5). God's omnipotent and supreme power is well able to keep the believer's faith secure.

Jesus declares that His sheep (those who are saved) will "never perish" (John 3:16). "Never" means never. In Philippians 1:6, Paul affirms that God will see through until its completion in heaven the saving work He initiated in the believer. John 10:28-29 presents the strongest proof for eternal security, stating that a believer cannot be snatched out of the encompassing hand of God.

> *"At conversion the believer is joined to the body of Christ by the Baptism of the Holy Spirit. If salvation can be lost, then one would have to be severed from the body and Christ's body would then be dismembered."*[20]
>
> —Charles Ryrie

Christians can and do sin (1 John 2:1) because of the dualistic nature in us—the flesh (carnal) and the spirit (spiritual). These two wrestle each other, competing for dominion throughout the believer's life. It is when the believer yields to the carnal nature that he or she sins, and although divine discipline may come for the rebellious act, the Christian's salvation is never in jeopardy (Romans 8:1). The Apostle Paul experienced this inner struggle like every other Christian (Romans 7:15-25) and discovered that the appetites of the flesh can only be thwarted by walking in the fullness of the Holy Spirit (Romans 8:1-11). To experience the victorious Christian life, believers must repudiate the flesh every day (1 Corinthians 15:31) and surrender again to the controlling influence of the

Holy Spirit (Ephesians 5:17). In addition, believers must be deliberate in "sowing" to the Spirit (Galatians 6:8) so that he or she may "reap" the fruit of the Spirit. Sowing to the Spirit involves cultivating and implementing lifestyle practices which please the Lord. Paul is clear that a person will reap what is sown (Galatians 6:7).

> "Walk in the Spirit (Galatians 5:16). All believers have the presence of the indwelling Holy Spirit (cf. Romans 8:9; 1 Corinthians 6:19, 20) as the personal power for living to please God. The form of the Greek verb translated 'walk' indicates continuous action, or a habitual lifestyle. Walking also implies progress; as a believer submits to the Spirit's control—that is, responds in obedience to the simple commands of Scripture—he grows in his spiritual life."[21]
> —John MacArthur

A native attempting to explain to a missionary the inner struggles of the flesh warring against the spirit said it was like two dogs fighting constantly. When asked which dog wins, the native replied, "The one I feed the most." In the warfare of the soul against the flesh "the one you feed the most" will win. Feed the good dog so it becomes a Great Dane, and starve the bad dog so it becomes a Chihuahua. It is up to us whether we cultivate good or bad habits.

But be clear about this: Eternal security does not convey a license to sin (Romans 6:15). The person who is genuinely saved both desires and delights in avoiding sin and is crushed deeply when he or she commits sin. In reality, many who profess to be saved but live contrary to the teaching of the Bible are not truly saved (Matthew 7:22-23) but are merely members of the visible church rather than the invisible Church. The Apostle John writes of such people: "They went out from us, but they were not of us; for if they had been of us, they would no doubt have continued with us: but they went out, that they might be made manifest that they were not all of us" (1 John 2:19).

> "Sometimes the regenerate backslides and falls into gross sin. But in this they act out of character, do violence to their own new nature, and make themselves deeply miserable, so that eventually they seek and find restoration to righteousness."[22]
> —J. I. Packer

REVIEW

(1) Even if Satan attacks a believer's faith, he can never _____ it.

(2) Why does Charles Ryrie say the idea of a believer losing his or her salvation makes no sense? _____

(3) What two "natures" fight for control of the believer's life? _____ and _____

(4) Even though a Christian cannot lose his or her salvation, what should motivate a believer to avoid sin? _____

BELIEVE THIS—*About the Holy Spirit*

The enabling and illuminating power source of the Christian's life is the Holy Spirit (Acts 1:8), the third person of the Trinity. The Holy Spirit resides in the believer (1 Corinthians 3:16–17; 6:19–20), helping the believer to pray (Romans 8:26–27), to avoid doing wrong (Galatians 5:16), to tell others of Jesus (Acts 1:8), to understand the Bible (1 Corinthians 2:6–16), to live in peace and joy (Romans 5:5), to know comfort in sorrow and difficulty (John 14:16–17), and to discern the will of God (Job 32:8; 33:4).

There is only one baptism of the Holy Spirit—and that occurs at conversion—but there can and should be many infillings of the Holy Spirit throughout the Christian's life (Ephesians 5:18). Upon baptism of the Holy Spirit at salvation, the Spirit takes up residence in the Christian.

> *"Meanwhile, they beg us {the apostles} not to grieve the Spirit, but rather to walk in the Spirit and to go on being filled with the Spirit.... But never, not once, do they exhort and instruct us to 'be baptized with the Spirit'. There can be only one explanation of this, namely that they are writing to Christians, and Christians have already been baptized with the Holy Spirit."*[23]
> —John Stott

The infilling of the Holy Spirit, then, takes place as the Christian yields to His control, allowing Him not only to be resident but President in his or her life (Galatians 5:16, 25). Referring to the infilling of the Holy Spirit, Leonard Ravenhill observes, "An automobile will never move until it has ignition-fire; so some men are neither moved nor moving because they have everything but fire."[24] The Holy Spirit "fires the engine" in a Christian's devotion, duty, and discipline.

C.H. Spurgeon summarizes the place of the Holy Spirit in the life of a believer:

> God has provided the Holy Spirit to guide us (John 16:13). The Holy Spirit is infallible. He knows everything and cannot lead us astray. He is ever-present. When we have no commentator or minister to help us, we still have the Holy Spirit. The Holy Spirit teaches us in three ways: suggestion, direction and illumination. There are thoughts that dwell in our minds that are suggestions put there by the Spirit for us to follow. Sometimes He leads us by direction, leading our thoughts along into a more excellent channel than that which we started. Sometimes He leads us by illuminating the Word of God to us.[25]

BELIEVE THIS!
UNIT 1

> "'Be filled' (Ephesians 5:18) is not a tentative suggestion, a mild recommendation, a polite piece of advice. It is a command which comes to us from Christ with all the authority of one of his chosen apostles. We have no more liberty to escape this duty than we have the ethical duties which surround the text, e.g. to speak the truth, to do honest work, to be kind and forgiving to one another, or to live lives of purity and love. The fullness of the Holy Spirit is not optional for the Christian, but obligatory."[26]
>
> —John Stott

REVIEW

(1) In what ways does the Holy Spirit help the believer live an effective Christian life? _____

(2) The _____ in the Holy Spirit takes place in the believer at the moment of salvation. The _____ with the Holy Spirit takes place at various times throughout a Christian's life.

(3) Distinguish how the Holy Spirit leads through suggestion, direction, and illumination. _____

BELIEVE THIS—*About Last Things*

An airline passenger may purchase either a one-way ticket or a two-way ticket. Obviously, the first indicates the passenger's desire to remain at the ticketed destination while the latter shows his desire to visit the ticketed destination but to return to the originating city at a stated time and date. John tells us Jesus came to earth with a *two-way ticket* (Revelation 22:20). The time and date for Jesus' return for the Church is set but known only to God: "But of that day and hour knoweth no man, no, not the angels of heaven, but my Father only" (Matthew 24:36). What we know specifically is that Jesus promised to return for His bride, the church of the redeemed (John 14:1–6).

There are 329 references to the Second Coming in the Bible. One of every 25 verses in the New Testament reference this event (for example, Matthew 24:30; 2 Thessalonians 1:7-8; Matthew 25:31; 1 Thessalonians 5:2-3; Matthew 25:31; Titus 2:13; Matthew 24:42 -51; and 1 Thessalonians 4:13-18). With regard to Jesus' Second Coming, the Bible reveals three key events as part of the overall drama of Christ's return.

GROWING IN KNOWLEDGE, LIVING BY FAITH
UNIT 1

(1) The Rapture (1 Thessalonians 4:13-18; 1 Corinthians 15:51-58)

"Rapture" means "to seize quickly or suddenly; to transport to a state of happiness." In Scripture, the Rapture occurs upon Jesus' return for His bride. It is the "catching up" to heaven of the saints and making complete their salvation. The first to be taken to Christ in the air are the saved who have already died. Then, the living saints will be caught up: "For the Lord himself shall descend from heaven with a shout, with the voice of the archangel, and with the trump of God: and the dead in Christ shall rise first: Then we which are alive and remain shall be caught up together with them in the clouds, to meet the Lord in the air: and so shall we ever be with the Lord" (1 Thessalonians 4:16-17).

(2) The Second Coming of Christ

There are two phases of the coming of Christ. The first is the Rapture in which Jesus comes for the saints and meets them in the air. At this time, believers will be changed in a twinkling of an eye to be like Jesus (1 Corinthians 15:51-52), receive rewards at the Judgment Seat (1 Corinthians 4:5), and partake of the Marriage Supper of the Lamb (Revelation 19:7–10). In the second phase, Jesus comes with His saints to earth to set up His Kingdom of 1000 years, known as the millennium reign (Revelation 19:11–15).

> *"I have felt like working three times as hard ever since I came to understand that my Lord was coming back again."*[27]
> —D. L. Moody

(3) The Judgment of Saint and Sinner

There will be a day when the people who love Jesus and those who do not will face God's judgment. In every courtroom in America, there is a judge who sits on a bench and makes people accept responsibility for their actions. God will do the same for all people (Hebrews 9:27). The Bible does not teach a general judgment for all mankind. It describes two judgments—one for the believer (Judgment Seat of Christ, 2 Corinthians 5:9-10) and one for the unbeliever (Great White Throne, Revelation 20:11-15). The Christian is not judged with regard to salvation because his soul is eternally secured through the blood of Christ. Rather, the Christian is judged in regard to conduct and service (1 Corinthians 3:11-15). This judgment determines a person's reward in heaven (Revelation 22:12; 4:10). The Bible states at least five rewards the believer may receive:

- The Crown of Life—for the persecuted saint who endures suffering for the cause of Christ (Revelation 2:10);
- The Crown of Rejoicing—for the soulwinner (1 Thessalonians 2:19; Philippians 4:1);
- The Crown of Righteousness—for believers who look for Jesus' return (2 Timothy 4:8);
- The Crown of Glory—for pastors who faithfully proclaim Christ and Him crucified, feed the flock of God, exhibit spiritual oversight for the flock of God, and lead by worthy example (1 Peter 5:1-4);
- The Incorruptible Crown—for the believer who, like an athlete, disciplines the body into subjection to Christ and becomes victorious over the flesh and who faithfully runs the Christian race to the finish line (1 Corinthians 9:24-27).

John declares that the believer can forfeit his or her reward (2 John 8) by failing to run the race by the rules presented in the Word of God. At the Great White Throne, the unbeliever will be judged according to his sin and rejection of Christ as Lord and Savior and will receive the condemnation of eternal torment in hell (Revelation 21:8).

> *"Heaven will not be the boring experience of strumming a harp on a cloud, as some facetiously characterize it. It will be the most dynamic, expanding, exhilarating experience conceivable. Our problem now is that, with our finite minds, we cannot imagine it."*[28]
> —Paul E. Little

HEAVEN AND HELL
Significant to an understanding of Christ's Second Coming, the Bible speaks of two literal places where people will spend eternity—heaven and hell (Luke 16: 22-23).

Seven important "R" words depict what sort of place heaven is.

(1) A place of Reception by Jesus. Jesus, not an angel, will greet and meet the believer at heaven's door (John 14:3).
(2) A place of Reunion with saints. The saint will fellowship not only with redeemed parents, children, grandparents and friends but also with all other redeemed people not known to the believer during life on earth. This includes the prophets, disciples, patriarchs, missionaries, and evangelists (1 Corinthians 13:12).
(3) A place of Release. It is "Hallelujah Square" because everybody is healthy and happy, freed from the grip of pain, sickness, crippling illness, suffering, and the constant pull of Satan toward sin (Revelation 21:4).
(4) A place of Rest. It has been said a person enters this world crying and goes out sighing. The saint gets tired and worn with the demands of livelihood and battling the foes of darkness, but "a day of rest" (Hebrews 4:9) is coming for the redeemed when he "will lay his sword down by the riverside and study war no more." A Christian works, knowing the labor will end with eternal rest in the Father's presence.
(5) A place of Rejoicing (Revelation 5:11-12). In heaven, the saint's joy will overflow into songs of praise and adoration to the King for making salvation possible. On earth, mankind is plagued with troubles and disappointments that rob joy and peace, but heaven is different.
(6) A place of Reward (Revelation 22:12), as noted in the section "The Judgment of Saint and Sinner" above.
(7) A place of Responsibility. Heaven is a place not only of worship but also of work. Christians will serve God in various ways for all eternity (Revelation 22:3).

> *"It is a sweet thing to die in the Lord....Death is no longer banishment, it is a return from exile, a going home to the many mansions where the loved ones already dwell."*[29]
> —C. H. Spurgeon

GROWING IN KNOWLEDGE, LIVING BY FAITH

UNIT 1

Hell is the complete opposite, and God does not desire anyone to go there (2 Peter 3:9). Jesus' story of the rich man and Lazarus reveals the sordid nature of hell (Luke 16:19-31) and reflects the six "P" words which we can use to describe hell.

(1) *A place of Pain.* Unimaginable physical and mental torment will be experienced in hell. There will be varying degrees of punishment in hell (Matthew 10:15; 11:22, 24; Mark 6:11; Hebrews 10:29).

(2) *A place of Passion.* Insatiable appetites and desires plague the inhabitants of hell.

(3) *A place of Parting.* The unsaved are separated forever from the redeemed.

(4) *A place of Prayer.* The eternally damned will come to see the need of God but too late. People in hell will weep, wail, and gnash their teeth, crying out to God for salvation—but in vain.

(5) *A place of Permeating Darkness.* Jude describes hell as "the blackness of darkness forever" (Jude 13). Utter blackness makes relationships impossible in hell. C. S. Lewis declares hell is a place of "nothing but yourself for all eternity!" The inhabitants of hell know only isolation and loneliness. There are no friendships or fellowship.

(6) *A place of Permanence.* Hell has no exits. There is no way out so there is no hope for its inhabitants. Yet, the worst aspect of hell is that God is not there!

> "A man's usefulness or uselessness depends upon what he believes and the stand he takes on the facts of Hell. But a man who accepts that part of the Bible which he wants to accept and which he calls agreeable to his thinking, and rejects that part which he does not want to accept, in plain, unvarnished language, is a fool!"[30]
> —R. A. Torrey

REVIEW

(1) What are the three key events in the Second Coming of Christ? _____

(2) What six "P" words describe hell? _____

(3) What are the five rewards for believers? _____

(4) What seven "R" words describe heaven? _____

(5) What six "P" words describe hell? _____

BELIEVE THIS!
UNIT 1

REFLECT—*Consider What This Means*

(1) Think about the last time you had an "Ah-ha!" experience about something. Briefly describe it: _____ Since God is omniscient, He never has "Ah-ha" moments, but He delights in yours. He wants you to discover new and exciting things about Himself and the world He's made.

(2) "You can't be two places at once" is a very human idea that makes complete sense to us, but it's not true of God. Picture someplace you've been before (other than where you are right now). Think about the fact that God is there right now and has been ever since you left it.

(3) Have you ever wondered whether or not the sun will come up tomorrow? Probably not. That's how sure you can be that God will always "be there" and will always be the same for you.

(4) What makes the Bible trustworthy? _____
_____
_____

(5) What is Satan's purpose and how does that affect you? _____
_____
_____
_____

(6) How does Jesus' teaching on Eternal Security motivate you to live a better Christian life? _____
_____
_____
_____

(7) What is the role of the Holy Spirit in your life? _____
_____

(8) How does the biblical perspective of Last Things affect you? _____
_____

(9) "If we believe the Bible, we cannot concede that other religions might be true as well. If we believe that Christ is Lord of all, and if we truly love Him, we cannot countenance the doctrines of those who deny Him (1 Corinthians 16:22). Christianity, if true at all, is exclusively true. Inherent in the claims of Christ is the assertion that He alone offers truth, and all religious systems that deviate from His truth are false. Jesus said, 'I am the way, the truth, and the life; no one comes to the Father, but through me.' (John 14:6) If this is true, every other religion is a lie. (Romans 3:4)"[31] —John MacArthur

How do the teachings explained in this unit support MacArthur's contention that Christianity is the only true religion? _____
_____
_____
_____
_____
_____
_____

GROWING IN KNOWLEDGE, LIVING BY FAITH

UNIT 1

RESPOND—*What Will You Do with What You Know?*

"Many suppose that intellectual freedom is identical with 'free thought', that is, the liberty to think and believe absolutely anything you want to think and believe. But this is not freedom. To believe nothing is to be in bondage to meaninglessness. To believe lies is to be in bondage to falsehood. True intellectual freedom is found in believing the truth and living by it."[32] —John Stott

(1) After studying the truths described in this unit, what adjustments do you need to make in your thinking? _____

(2) What lies have you fallen prey to? _____

(3) Are there any thoughts or attitudes you've adopted in the name of "intellectual freedom" that you need to change? _____

(4) Read one of these books:
   A Survey of Bible Doctrine, Charles C. Ryrie
   What Baptists Believe, Herschel H. Hobbs
   Know What You Believe, Paul Little
   The Popular Bible Prophecy Commentary, Tim LaHaye and Ed Hindson
   Systematic Theology (Volumes 1-4), Norman Geisler

UNIT 2

THE NEW BIRTH

"The doctrine of the New Birth upsets all false religion—all false views about the Bible and about God."[33]
—D. L. Moody

*"I wish that there were some wonderful place
Called the Land of Beginning Again,
Where all our mistakes and all our heartaches
Could be dropped like a shabby old coat at the door"*[34]
—Louisa Fletcher

In the classic poem "The Land of Beginning Again," the writer longs for a land where she can lay aside the past, much as a man puts aside soiled clothes to start fresh. Although in the poem this "Land of Beginning Again" is make-believe, for Christians there is such a place found in a personal relationship with Jesus Christ. The Bible calls the refreshing new beginning "the new birth." This spiritual birth requires "repentance and faith" (Acts 20:21).

As noted in Unit 1, repentance is godly sorrow over wrongdoing, coupled with a desire to change. Faith is belief in the fact and meaning of Jesus' death, burial, and resurrection, and it is the receiving of Jesus into a person's life as both Savior and Lord (Romans 10: 9-13). Based on these two conditions of salvation, at the time of sincere prayer to receive Christ as Lord and Savior, a sinner is "born again"(Romans 10:13; Revelation 3:20).

> **WORD WISDOM: BORN AGAIN, NEW BIRTH**
>
> Renewal of a person's spiritual condition that occurs at the moment a sinner confesses Jesus as Lord and Savior and exhibits repentance and faith (*Acts 20:21; John 3:3; 1 Peter 1:23*). It results in a radical change in conscience, conduct, and conviction (*2 Corinthians 5:17*).

C. H. Spurgeon described the nature of this unseen but very real experience:

> This great work is supernatural. It is not an operation which a man performs for himself: a new principle is infused, which works in the heart, renews the soul, and affects the entire man. It is not a change of my name, but a renewal of my nature, so that I am not the man I used to be, but a new man in Christ Jesus.[35]

Prior to the Civil War, Abraham Lincoln purchased a beautiful young African-American woman at an auction. He immediately told her former master, "Remove her chains."
The woman asked Lincoln, "What ya' goin' to do wit' me now?"
"Why, I am going to set you free."
"Free. What do ya mean, free?" she asked.
Mr. Lincoln replied, "I mean you are a free person. You are no longer a slave." And went on to explain that she could go wherever and do whatever she wanted.
To his shock, The lady exclaimed, "Then I want to be wit' you!" Puzzled, he eyed her and explained again, "You can go anywhere. Why would you want to follow me?"

GROWING IN KNOWLEDGE, LIVING BY FAITH
UNIT 2

The rescued woman answered, "Cause I wanna be wit' the one who set me free."

This touching story reflects a truth that happens with anyone who truly accepts and appreciates the salvation Jesus offers. Once people experience the deliverance of Jesus Christ from the power and penalty of sin, they feel toward Him the way the freed slave felt toward Abraham Lincoln.

REVIEW

(1) How is new birth like living in "The Land of Beginning Again"? _____
_____

(2) Spurgeon explains the unseen power of being born again by reminding us that it is a _____
_____ work.

(3) What are the "chains" Jesus removes when He sets a sinner free? _____
_____

RELIGION IS NOT A SUBSTITUTE FOR NEW BIRTH

Church attendance, moral living, religious service, baptism, and partaking of the Lord's Supper are not synonymous with the new birth. The believer does these things because he or she is a child of God, not in order to become a child of God.

In an article entitled "The Agonizing Problem of the Assurance of Salvation," John Piper raises a troubling question:

> This [new birth] boils down to whether I have saving faith. What makes this agonizing for many in the history of the church and today is that there are people who think they have saving faith but don't (Matthew 7:21-22). So the agonizing question for some is: Do I really have saving faith? Is my faith real? Am I self-deceived?[36]

Piper points out that, in order to gain assurance of their salvation, many sincere, well-meaning people wrongly believe faith is a mere decision to affirm biblical truths (e.g., Jesus is the Son of God who died for man's sin) or that faith requires no life-change to demonstrate its reality. "But these strategies to help assurance backfire," says Piper. "And, perhaps worst of all, they sometimes give assurance to people who should not have it."[37]

Possessing a *false hope* of salvation is just as damning as having *no hope*. Jesus warns:

> Not every one that saith unto me, Lord, Lord, shall enter into the kingdom of heaven; but he that doeth the will of my Father which is in heaven. Many will say to me in that day, "Lord, Lord, have we not prophesied in thy name? and in thy name have cast out devils? and in thy name done many wonderful works?" And then will I profess unto them, "I never knew you: depart from me, ye that work iniquity" (Matthew 7: 21–23).

Salvation is totally based upon Christ's work for the sinner at Calvary. Man cannot add to it in even the smallest way. God's promises assure us of new birth (1 John 1:9; Titus 1:2).

THE FACT, NOT FEELING, OF SALVATION

Feelings are not proof of salvation. The proof of salvation rests upon God's Word. While the believer certainly should feel relief that things are eternally settled with God and should feel awesome gratitude to God, validating salvation by emotional experiences is not biblical (Romans 8:16). Fact, faith, and feeling are like a steam locomotive train. Fact is the engine that pulls the train, faith is the boiler that fuels the engine, and feeling is the caboose. The train must have an engine and boiler to function, but the caboose is optional.

> *"I believe in heartfelt religion, and thank God for the joy He gives day by day. However, nowhere in the Bible can we find information on how one must feel before he is saved or after he is saved. Feeling varies with the person saved."*[38]
> —John R. Rice

THE THREE VERB TENSES OF SALVATION

Salvation takes place in three tenses:

(1) The believer has been saved from the guilt and penalty of sin (1 Corinthians 1:18; Luke 7:50). Salvation occurs in an instant upon repentance and faith expressed to the Lord Jesus Christ.

(2) The believer is being saved from the habit and dominion of sin (Romans 6:14; Philippians 2:12-13). Solomon compares the believer's progression in sanctification to the sun: "But the path of the just is as the shining light, that shineth more and more unto the perfect day" (Proverbs 4:18). The Christian is saved in an instant (sunrise) but godliness is progressive (as the sun rises in the sky) until clothed with Christ's perfection in heaven (sun reaches noonday). A grave contradiction exists when one states the fact of personal salvation and yet is content to continue in the old life of sin (2 Corinthians 5:17).

(3) The believer will be saved to absolute, total conformity to Christ in "the perfect day" (Proverbs 4:18; Romans 13:11). A day is coming when the saint's transformation into the likeness of Christ will be complete (1 John 3:2).

REVIEW

(1) In which of the three tenses of salvation do church attendance, moral living, religious service, baptism, and partaking of the Lord's Supper fit? _____

(2) Read Romans 8:16 and explain why it teaches that something other than feelings give assurance of the believer's right standing with God. _____

(3) Answer "yes" or "no": Have you been saved? _____. Are you being saved? _____. Will you be saved? _____.

THE ASSURANCE OF SALVATION

Your assurance of salvation must be based soundly upon God's Word to you, God's Work for you, and God's Witness in you.

God's Word to You. "These things have I written unto you that believe on the name of the Son of God; that ye may know that ye have eternal life, and that ye may believe on the name of the Son of God" (1 John 5:13). Unlike John's Gospel that is written specifically to win the lost, the Epistle of First John is written to saints to assure them of eternal life based on the promises of the Word of God. The bottom line concerning salvation is what God says in Holy Scripture (Romans 10:9-13; John 3:16; Acts 20:21).

> *"He is the Great Physician and will heal our souls instantly if we will trust Him. As we would trust a doctor, submit to his treatment and depend on him for results, so we should trust Jesus today regarding our souls."*[39]
> —John R. Rice

> *"The voice of sin may be loud, but the voice of forgiveness is louder."*[40]
> —D. L. Moody

God's Work for You. Jesus died on the cross and was raised from the dead to make salvation possible. The instant a person invites Christ into his or her life, Jesus' work of reconciliation and regeneration takes place. These scripture texts reveal Christ's work in the life of the sinner at the moment of salvation regarding sins:

- He takes them away (John 1:29);
- He forgets them (Hebrews 10:17);
- He washes them away (Isaiah 1:17-18);
- He blots them out (Isaiah 43:25);
- He wipes them out like a cloud (Isaiah 44:22);
- He pardons them (Isaiah 55:7);
- He buries them in the depths of the sea (Micah 7:19);
- He separates them from the sinner as far as the east is from the west (Psalm 103:12).

The Old Testament provides a remarkable illustration of the work of Christ. In Israel on the Day of Atonement, the high priest placed his hands upon the head of a flawless goat and confessed the sins of the people, symbolically transferring their sin to the goat. This "scapegoat"—sin-bearer—of the people was led into a remote part of the desert and let loose where it would never be found (Leviticus 16:20-22). This Old Testament scapegoat expresses New Testament atonement: Jesus Christ is the Supreme Scapegoat, provided by God to forgive sin and bear it into the "desert" of everlasting forgetfulness.

THE NEW BIRTH
UNIT 2

> *My sins were laid on Jesus,*
> *The spotless Lamb of God;*
> *He bore them all and freed me*
> *From the accursed load.*
> *My guilt was borne by Jesus;*
> *He cleansed the crimson stains*
> *In His own blood most precious*
> *And not a spot remains.*[41]
>
> —Horatius Bonar

God's Witness in Me. There are two ways God gives witness to His presence in the believer.
(1) The witness of the Holy Spirit. At conversion, the Holy Spirit takes up residence in the believer's heart and assures the believer that he or she has passed from death to life: "The Spirit itself beareth witness with our spirit that we are the children of God" (Romans 8:16).
(2) The witness of a changed life. Conversion results in change (2 Corinthians 5:17). It is impossible for a born again believer to remain the same in conscience, conviction, and conduct. The way a person views these things changes. An old African-American saying makes this point: "The day I got saved, my feet got a brand new walk, and my speech got a brand new talk." A difference occurs at salvation that continues to progress throughout a Christian's life.

One of my all-time gospel favorites is "It's Different Now," a David Beatty hymn that proclaims this biblical truth:

> It's different now since Jesus saved my soul
> It's different now since Jesus made me whole
> Ole Satan had to flee when Jesus rescued me
> Now it's different, oh so different now.[42]

Vance Havner explains the extreme devotion we owe to Christ:

> We only have one option: we can receive the Lord or reject Him. But once we receive Him, our option ends. We are no longer our own but bought with a price. We belong to Him. He has the first word and the last. He demands absolute loyalty beyond that of any earthly dictator but He has the right to do it. "Love so amazing, so divine, demands my soul, my life, my all." How foolish to say, "Nobody is going to tell me how much to give, what to do." We have already been told! We are His and His Word is final....I came to Christ as a country boy. I did not understand all about the plan of salvation. One does not have to understand it; he has only to stand on it. But one thing I did understand even as a lad: I understood that I was under new management. I belonged to Christ and He was Lord.[43]

Havner is right on target. Genuine salvation results in transference of ownership of self to Jesus Christ. We no longer belong to ourselves for we have been bought with a great price. Jesus is now Lord of our lives.

God's Word makes the believer sure, God's Work makes the believer safe, and God's Witness makes the believer secure. As Spurgeon points out:

> [Satan] tells us most assuredly we cannot be saved. Remember, sinner, it is not thy hold of Christ that saves thee – it is Christ; it is not thy joy in Christ that saves thee – it is Christ; it is not even faith in Christ, though that is the instrument – it is Christ's blood and merits; therefore look not so much to thy hand with which thou art grasping Christ as to Christ; look not to thy hope, but to Christ, the source of thy hope; look not to thy faith; and if thou do that, ten thousand devils can not throw thee down, but as long as thou lookest at thyself, the meanest of those evil spirits may tread thee beneath his feet.[44]

> **WORD WISDOM: REGENERATION**
>
> A change of being, a passing from death unto life brought about by the work of the Holy Spirit, literally "The New Birth" (*John 1:12-13*).

> My hope is built on nothing less than Jesus' blood and righteousness.
> I dare not trust the sweetest frame, but wholly lean on Jesus' name.
>
> On Christ the solid rock I stand, all other ground is sinking sand;
> all other ground is sinking sand.
> —Edward Mote, 1797-1874

So, never be ashamed of the decision to become a Christian (Romans 1:16; Matthew 10:32-33).

GOD'S HAND IN THE GLOVE OF YOUR LIFE

To live a victorious Christian life, the believer must constantly abide in Christ (John 15:5). To abide in Christ means to keep Him at the center of life, to obey Him without vacillating, to take cues from Him regarding decisions and conduct, and to steadfastly walk in intimacy with Him. Abiding in Christ requires serious diligence in the spiritual disciplines. Recall the illustration shared in the Introduction regarding the two methods of making tea. The victorious believer cannot be a dipper spiritually—dipping in and out of the Word, church, prayer, service, purity, obedience, and communion with the Lord but must abide (stay put) in these disciplines.

> *"Alka-Seltzer Christians fizzle for a little while and disappear."*[45]
> —Adrian Rogers

Envision a baseball glove on the ground. If a fly ball or grounder is hit right to the glove, could it make the catch? Obviously not. The glove cannot fulfill its purpose unless a baseball player's hand is in the glove. Properly fitted on a hand—abiding in it—that glove immediately becomes capable of anything the ballplayer can do. Your life is like the glove. Apart from the hand of God inserted in your life, it accomplishes nothing. However, with God's hand abiding in the glove of your life, you can do anything God designs.

And just as dirt in a finger of the glove prevents the ball player's full control in its use, dirt in the believer's life hinders its use by God. Keep the glove clean and well oiled for His use, 24/7. You must "stay put" in Jesus to experience the victorious Christian life and the great and mighty things He will do through you.

THE NEW BIRTH

UNIT 2

REVIEW

(1) What is the assurance of salvation founded on? _____

(2) List eight things that happen to sin at the moment of salvation: _____

(3) What does the Old Testament "scapegoat" represent? _____

(4) What are the two "witnesses" of God in the life of the believer? _____

(5) List several aspects of what it means to abide in Christ. _____

WORD WISDOM: SALVATION

Salvation is a sinner's state of being once he or she has been delivered from the penalty and power of sin. In Heaven, this even includes being removed from the presence of sin Salvation comes about only by the intervention of God through His Son Jesus Christ (*Acts 4:12; Titus 2:11*).

NEGLECT NOT: SALVATION

How shall we escape, if we neglect so great salvation; which at the first began to be spoken by the Lord.

—Hebrews 2:3

The writer of Hebrews exhorts "Neglect not so great salvation." This first "neglect not" of Scripture lays the essential foundation for putting into practice all the others.

Perhaps you have considered making a decision for Christ, but so far you have not taken action. I encourage you to stop putting it off and offer "repentance toward God and faith in the Lord Jesus Christ" (Acts 20:21). The door of opportunity to be saved is wide open presently, but it can shut without warning. As James cautions, "What is your life? It's but a vapor that appeareth for a little time and then passeth away" (James 4:14). Your end may come unexpectedly. Many of the "statistics" we hear about in the news are people who had no idea their last day was upon them. So please hear the urgency of the Hebrews 2:3 question: "How shall you escape?"

If you neglect the salvation of God through Jesus, how do you expect to escape a wasted life, wasted influence, emptiness, meaninglessness, and, ultimately, eternal damnation in hell? Have you thought about what that means for you. The answer to the question is that there is no way to escape these things apart from a relationship with Jesus Christ. If you've been neglectful, please Neglect Not this great invitation to be saved by a gracious Lord any longer. Join the family of God now by receiving Jesus as Lord and Savior (see #3 in the "Respond" section at the end of this unit).

GROWING IN KNOWLEDGE, LIVING BY FAITH
UNIT 2

Salvation is a good word; it denotes that comprehensive purpose of God by which he justifies, sanctifies, and glorifies his people: first pardoning their offences and accepting them as righteous in his sight; then progressively transforming them by his Spirit into the image of Christ, until finally they become like Christ in heaven, when they see him as he is, and their bodies are raised incorruptible like Christ's body of glory."[46]

—H. F. Stevenson

REFLECT—*Consider What This Means*

(1) Write on a piece of paper your story—how you came to realize a personal need of new birth and to be saved. Share date, place, and circumstances.

(2) How do you know that you are a Christian? _____

(3) What role do feelings play in salvation? _____

(4) What are the two conditions of salvation? _____

RESPOND—*What Will You Do with What You Know?*

(1) A man risked his life swimming through dangerous rip tides to rescue a young man. Catching his breath, the boy said to his rescuer, "Thank you for saving me." The man responded, "That's okay, kid. Just make sure your life was worth saving."
May all the ransomed of God who were rescued from the rip tides of eternal condemnation by Jesus "make sure their life was worth saving."
   • What are you doing for Christ to make sure your life "was worth saving"? _____

(2) People accept the witness (word) of pharmacists regarding medicines, bankers regarding bank statements, and the US Treasury regarding the value of a dollar. The Apostle John emphatically declares that "the witness (word) of God is greater (more sure, certain, reliable)" than that of man (1 John 5:9). Do you have a harder time accepting God's Word than that of other people you trust? _____
What will you do, starting today, to commit yourself to accepting and acting on God's Word to you? _____

(3) If you have been "neglecting" the great salvation described in this unit, stop neglecting it, and pray to receive Christ right now. The prayer noted below has been used by many to ask Jesus to become Savior and Lord. Use it to come to Christ in faith, and add any specific confessions of sin you feel a need to share with the Lord.

> *Lord Jesus, I am a sinner in need of Your forgiveness. I am sorry for breaking Your Law and for my disobedience. Thank You for dying on the Cross and being raised from the dead to make my salvation possible. I do invite You into my life to be Lord and Savior. Amen*

UNIT 3

THE SIGNIFICANCE OF THE BIBLE

No Spiritual Discipline is more important than the intake of God's Word. Nothing can substitute for it. There simply is no healthy Christian life apart from a diet of the milk and meat of Scripture.[47]
—Donald S. Whitney

Now the measure in which we profit from our reading and study of Scriptures may be ascertained by the extent to which Christ is becoming more real and more precious unto our hearts.[48]
—A. W. Pink

At Yellowstone National Park each winter, dozens of young bears die while waiting along the highway for a handout after tourist season has ended. No one comes to feed them, and they starve to death.

Christians must not be like the overly dependent bears, waiting for others to instruct them about Jesus, or they will starve spiritually (2 Timothy 2:15). Personal spiritual growth depends on the intake of God's Word. As food is vital for the body's growth, God's Word is for the soul's growth. Peter teaches that a spiritual baby in Christ needs feeding to grow up into spiritual maturity just as a baby needs feeding in order to grow up into an adult (1 Peter 2:2).

The reading and study of Scripture promotes Christian growth in at least five ways:

- It reveals sin. The Holy Scripture uses Scripture itself to shine light on the dirt in a person's heart (Psalm 119:130).
- It sanctifies (cleanses) its recipient (Hebrews 4:12).
- It protects. The Psalmist declares, "Wherewithal shall a young man cleanse his way? By giving heed to the word of God" (Psalm 119:9).
- It repels sin, purifying and preserving power in the life of the saint. David said, "Thy word have I hid in my heart that I may not sin against thee" (Psalm 119:11).
- It instructs, "that the man of God may be perfect, thoroughly furnished ('equipped') unto all good works" (2 Timothy 3:17).

A person does not need to look outside the Bible for theological guidance about holy living. Scripture not only tells the Christian how to live but supplies the means to live the life it espouses (1 Corinthians 4:6). George Mueller, a nineteenth century pastor in England, understood the central importance of Scripture for growth in Christ:

> I saw that the most important thing I had to do was give myself to the reading of the Word of God—not

WORD WISDOM: INSPIRATION

"Inspiration" as used in 2 Timothy 3:16 does not mean that Scripture is inspiring to read—though it is—but that it is divinely "breathed out" of the heart of God. It originated in its totality with God (*Matthew 4:4; Luke 4:4*).

prayer, but the Word of God. Here again, not the simple reading of the Word of God so that it only passes through my mind just as water runs through a pipe, but considering what I read, pondering over it, and applying it to my heart. To meditate on it, that thus my heart might be comforted, encouraged, warned, reproved, instructed. And that thus, by means of the Word of God, while meditating on it, my heart be brought into experiencing Communion with the Lord.[49]

HOW DO WE KNOW THE BIBLE IS RELIABLE?

While the Bible validates itself through an array of "internal" supports of its reliability—consistency, multiple witnesses, verifiable history—the Bible is also validated by many "external" evidences. For instance, it has been confirmed by more than one hundred archaeological finds. To mention a few:

- At one time scholars dismissed as factual the existence and description of the Hittite nation until their capital and records were discovered at Bogazkoy, Turkey.[50]
- Skeptics thought Solomon's wealth was greatly exaggerated until recent discoveries revealed that wealth in antiquity was concentrated with the king.[51]
- Some claimed that there was never an Assyrian king named Sargon (Isaiah 20:1) until his palace was discovered in Khorsabad, Iraq.[52]
- King Belshazzar (Daniel 5) also was counted to be fictitious until a find of tablets were found showing that he was Nabonidus' son who served as coregent in Babylon.[53]
- Outside the Bible, no documentation was known to give credence to the existence of Pontius Pilate. But in 1961, archeologists discovered at Caesarea a stone inscription that bore Pontius Pilate's inscription honoring the Roman emperor Tiberius. Coins have also been discovered dating from Pilate's gubernatorial rule.[54]
- Ruins in the synagogue at Capernium, where Jesus taught and of Peter's House in Capernium have been discovered. Archaeological evidence for the existence of Paul has been validated overwhelmingly by ruins in Cyprus, Galatia, Philippi, Thessalonica, Berea, Athens, Corinth, Ephesus, Rome, and surrounding areas. The rule of Herod the Great at the time of Jesus' birth is substantiated by the numerous excavations of his massive public works in the Holy Land, including the Great Temple in Jerusalem.[55]

> **WORD WISDOM: INFALLIBILITY, INERRANCY**
>
> The Bible is free from the liability to mislead, deceive, or err (*Psalm 12:6*). It is unmixed with errors in its original writing ("autograph" copy). Man's rejection or neglect of Holy Scripture does not alter its power to accomplish God's purposes (*Isaiah 55:11*).

The archaeologist's blade is ever confirming the Bible as truth and will continue to do so until the return of Christ.

The text of the Bible is itself a well-documented piece of antiquity. Discovery of the Dead Sea Scrolls in 1947 substantiated the integrity and accuracy of Scripture. Pastor and theologian W. A. Criswell explained the significance of the Dead Sea Scrolls in a sermon entitled "My Favorite Text":

THE SIGNIFICANCE OF THE BIBLE
UNIT 3

...if you've been to Israel, why, there's a Shrine of the Book in Jerusalem on the campus of the Hebrew university. And in that shrine you will see some of those Dead Sea Scrolls, one of which is the book of Isaiah, out of which I'm preaching. Now that book of Isaiah that you will see in Israel was written about 150 years before Christ. And the text, 150 years before Christ that you can look at is exactly like the text of the Masoretes, which was written between 900 and 1000 A.D. The significance of the Dead Sea Scrolls is this, mostly this: that the transmission of the Word of God has been faithful and true according to the careful preservation of the edict and mandate of God in heaven.[56]

> *"While the Christian can marshal good arguments from personal experience, science, archaeology, and prophecy, he cannot "prove" the Bible true and authoritative. Still, he knows the Bible is true because of his resident truth-teacher–the Holy Spirit. The Holy Spirit is the only One who can prove God's Word is true, and He does this as He works in the heart and mind of the Christian whom He indwells."* [57]
> —John MacArthur

While some people like to doubt the authenticity of the Bible, they ignore the historical fact that it is more well-documented than any other ancient writing, most of which people take for granted. The biblical text is better preserved and more thoroughly supported by scholarly evidence, for instance, than the writings of Plato and Aristotle.

REVIEW

(1) Reading and study of Scripture is as essential to _____ growth as eating is to _____ growth.

(2) Name five ways Bible study contributes to spiritual growth: _____

(3) List several examples of archaeological discoveries that demonstrate the accuracy and reliability of the Bible: _____

(4) What is the significance of the Dead Sea Scrolls? _____

(5) The Bible is more well-documented than any other ancient writings.   ❏True   ❏False

THE RIGHT APPROACH TO SCRIPTURE

D. L. Moody outlines four things a person must do to have the right mindset for studying the Bible:

- Admit its truth;
- Submit to its teachings;
- Commit it to memory;
- Transmit it to others.[58]

John Stott offers similar counsel:

> If we come to Scripture with our minds made up, expecting to hear from it only an echo of our own thoughts and never the thunderclap of God's, then indeed he will not speak to us

GROWING IN KNOWLEDGE, LIVING BY FAITH
UNIT 3

and we shall only be confirmed in our own prejudices. We must allow the Word of God to confront us, to disturb our security, to undermine our complacency and to overthrow our patterns of thought and behavior.[59]

> *If I were the devil, one of my first aims would be to stop folk from digging into the Bible.*[60]
> —J. I. Packer

Satan attempts to keep believers from taking Scripture seriously, but he can be thwarted through a disciplined regimen of Bible study. While we will explore several specific approaches to Bible study, any method will be improved by keeping in mind the following five keys to effective Bible study (Adapted from unknown source):

1. Study it through. Never start a day without "dissecting" a segment of Holy Scripture (Psalm 39:3).
2. Pray it in. "Digest" through prayer what you dissect.
3. Write it down. Record in a journal the truth and lessons gained from the text you study
4. Work it out. Throughout the day, flesh out the truth of the text.
5. Pass it on. Find ways to tell others what you learned in your Bible study.

> *The Bible is full of Truth. You can spend your whole life studying it, and it still will be fresh and wonderful.*[61]
> —John MacArthur

With any study method, it is crucial to make personal application of the scriptural text. As you study, ask these questions to keep your thoughts focused:

- What does this text reveal about Jesus?
- What is the context of the passage?
- What is the main lesson it teaches?
- In light of this text, what action should I take?

Whatever God makes paramount in His Word, He expects to be prominent in the life of the believer. Keep in mind that simply reading the Bible is not Bible study. True study involves dissection and application of a scripture. Max Lucado emphasizes this crucial component of effective Bible study

> *Search and you will find is the pledge.* The Bible is not a newspaper to be skimmed but rather a mine to be quarried. *Search for it like silver, and hunt for it like hidden treasure. Then you will understand respect for the LORD, and you will find that you know God* (Proverbs 2:4).[62]

To be fully open to whatever Scripture may speak to you, it is essential to set aside personal prejudices, convictions, and pre-conceived notions when approaching the Bible. You must allow the Word to speak freely for itself without the hindrance of predetermined interpretations or understanding.

THE SIGNIFICANCE OF THE BIBLE

UNIT 3

Because Christ is the fixed point of reference for theology, we are concerned with how the text relates to Christ and how we relate to Christ.[63]

—Graeme Goldsworthy

METHODS OF BIBLE STUDY

A Bible that is falling apart usually belongs to someone who isn't.
—Anonymous

Once you've determined to come to the Bible with a heart and mind open to instruction by the Holy Spirit, there are a number of refreshing and enjoyable means by which to dig into Scripture. I've outlined below eight respected methods you'll want to try.

1. *Read a Scripture passage repetitively.* Read a book of the Bible five times, and then begin to study it. Repetitive reading prior to actual study will result in clearer illumination of the text's theme. In initiating the study of a book of the Bible, A. T. Pearson suggests searching out five P's: place where written, person by whom written, people to whom written, purpose for which written, period at which written.[64] Next, summarize with a few sentences the central meaning of each chapter and how it applies to your life.

2. *Study the Bible thematically.* Study a theme such as "grace," "holiness," or "the second coming" by reading all the passages you can find on the subject.

3. *Study the Bible doctrinally.* Study a specific doctrine of the faith such as the "deity of Christ," "blood atonement," "the resurrection of Christ," or "judgment." Look up, and internalize passages that relate to your subject.

> **WORD WISDOM: PROPHECY**
>
> The prediction or forth telling of a divine event, prompted and governed by the Holy Spirit (*2 Peter 1:21; Revelation 22:18-19*); Spoken by prophets.

4. *Study the miracles of the Bible.* There are more than 120 miracles recorded in Scripture, including the miraculous haul of fish (Luke 5:4-11), the raising of the widow's son at Nain (Luke 7:11-18), the woman with the spirit of infirmity (Luke 13:11-17), the man with dropsy (Luke 14:1-6), the ten lepers (Luke 17:11-19), and the healing of Malchus (Luke 22:50-51).

5. *Study the parables.* Over one-third of Jesus' teaching in the Bible is comprised of parables. A parable is an earthly story or example that illustrates or teaches a spiritual truth. Jesus' parables include Matthew 7:24-28; 9:16-18; 11:16-17; 13:3-10; 13:24-31; 13:33; 13:44; Mark 4:26-29; Luke 6:39-42 and John 15:1-7.

6. *Study Biblical prophecy.* The study of prophecy undergirds and strengthens the believer's grasp on the authority of Scripture (2 Peter 1:19). Fulfilled prophecy is one of the marvelous internal evi-

> ## "HOW TO READ THE BIBLE"
> ### by C.H. Spurgeon
>
> We are not always fit, it seems to me, to read the Bible. At times it were well for us to stop before we open the volume. "Put off thy shoe from thy foot, for the place whereon thou standest is holy ground." You have just come in from careful thought and anxiety about your worldly business, and you cannot immediately take that book and enter into its heavenly mysteries. As you ask a blessing over your meat before you fall to, so it would be a good rule for you to ask a blessing on the word before you partake of its heavenly food. Pray the Lord to strengthen your eyes before you dare to look into the eternal light of Scripture. As the priests washed their feet at the laver before they went to their holy work, so it were well to wash the soul's eyes with which you look upon God's Word, to wash even the fingers, if I may so speak—the mental fingers with which you will turn from page to page—that with a holy book you may deal after a holy fashion. Say to your soul—"Come, soul, wake up: thou art not now about to read the newspaper; thou art not now perusing the pages of a human poet to be dazzled by his flashing poetry; thou art coming very near to God, who sits in the Word like a crowned monarch in his halls. Wake up, my glory; wake up, all that is within me. Though just now I may not be praising and glorifying God, I am about to consider that which should lead me so to do, and therefore it is an act of devotion. So be on the stir, my soul: be on the stir, and bow not sleepily before the awful throne of the Eternal." Scripture reading is our spiritual meal time. Sound the gong and call in every faculty to the Lord's own table to feast upon the precious meat which is now to be partaken of; or, rather, ring the church-bell as for worship, for the studying of the Holy Scripture ought to be as solemn a deed as when we lift the psalm upon the Sabbath day in the courts of the Lord's house.[65]

dences for the authenticity of Scripture. Most significantly, of the thirty different biblical prophecies concerning the birth, death, and resurrection of the Messiah, Jesus Christ fulfilled every one. To put that in perspective: The potential of Jesus fulfilling all thirty "by chance" is the same as the probability of flipping a quarter thirty times and having it land on heads all thirty times. Statisticians can show that it would require one billion people flipping coins to have just one end up with heads all thirty times. That's a lot of "heads in a row," isn't it? So prophecy affirms the deity of Christ, and studying prophecies will affirm your faith in Scripture.

> *We should certainly reject any claim that there are prophets today comparable to the biblical prophets. For they were the "mouth" of God, special organs of revelation, whose teaching belongs to the foundation on which the church is built.*[66]
>
> —John Stott

7. *Study great Bible words.* Study biblical words like "justification," "repentance," "glorification," and "sanctification." Look up verses that explain or demonstrate each word.

8. *Study by Scripture memory.* "Thy word have I hid in mine heart, that I might not sin against thee" (Psalm 119:11). Scripture verses will keep you from spiritual reverses. I have found it helpful to print out memory verses on cards small enough to put on a key ring. The verses can be taken

THE SIGNIFICANCE OF THE BIBLE
UNIT 3

wherever you go and reviewed consistently. This method also enables you to review verses previously learned while working on a new verse. For additional memorization ideas, check out the Navigators' excellent Scripture memory plan (www.navigators.org).

REVIEW

1) Who would like to keep you from serious study of Scripture? _____
(2) What are the five keys to effective Bible study, no matter what specific method you use? _____
_____
(3) What do you need to lay aside in order to hear clearly what God wants to say to you through Scripture study? _____
(4) What are the eight methods of Bible Study reviewed in this chapter? _____
_____

TOOLS FOR BIBLE STUDY

To competently dig into Scripture, a few tools are essential. Everyone should have in their library of helps at least these five:

- Bible dictionary—defines Bible words and serves as an encyclopedia on biblical subjects.
- Concordance—lists all the words in the Bible, references the texts in which they are found, and describes the original meaning of the Greek and Hebrew.
- Commentary—provides interpretation and explanation of biblical texts, sometimes including suggested sermon outlines.
- Journal—to record your own thoughts, impressions, and lessons learned.
- Study Bible—a complete Bible which also provides interpretive notes on many verses as well as other helps such as maps, articles, and timelines of historical events.

If you want to expand your library, other valuable study resources include the following:

- Bible atlas—to show geographical locations of Bible texts.
- Bible handbook—provides an overview of Bible books and chapters.
- Interlinear Bible—cites the Hebrew or Greek text between the lines of the English rendering.
- Lexicon—defines and explains background of Hebrew and Greek words.
- Topical Bible—lists Biblical texts that illuminate the meanings of key words.
- Word studies—gives background, original meaning, and cultural usage of biblical words.

The "Respond" section at the end of this unit provides recommendations for specific editions of these resources.

MAKE A PLACE FOR BIBLE STUDY

To support your personal discipline of Bible study, you will need to establish a specific place to do your work. It should be a secluded place, as free from interruptions and disturbances as possible. Since it is a place to meet the Creator of the world and your personal Savior, it should be a special

GROWING IN KNOWLEDGE, LIVING BY FAITH
UNIT 3

place where there is "no horsing around," a sacred place of awe and holiness where the "brush of angel wings are felt all around." Make sure, too, it can be a scheduled place where you will meet with God routinely, at the same time each day.

"Hurry" is the death of Bible study. Schedule adequate time to read and muse over a Scripture text, so you can sift from it all that it is ready to yield.

REVIEW

(1) What are the tools necessary for thorough Bible study? _____

(2) What is the significance of having a special place for Bible study? _____

(3) Scheduling ample time for Bible study is crucial because _____ is the death of Bible study.

REFLECT—*Consider What This Means*

(1) Are you nourishing yourself with God's Word, or are you waiting for a "handout" like the bears in Yellowstone National Park? _____ If so, imagine the renewed energy you feel after you've eaten a good meal and think about how taking better care to feed yourself spiritually would energize your spiritual life.

(2) It has been said that there are three stages of Bible study. Read the description of each below and consider which stage you are in. If you haven't made it to stage three yet, determine what you'll need to do to get there.
   1. Castor Oil Stage. You do your Bible study like taking bad tasting medicine because you know it is good for you, not because you really want to.
   2. Shredded Wheat Stage. You find Bible study dry and bland but nourishing.
   3. Peaches and Cream Stage. This is the stage where you really look forward to Bible Study. It is both a desire and delight.[67]

(3) Theologian John Stott said this about having the right approach to the Bible:
   Some honor the Word and neglect the Spirit who alone can interpret it; others honor the Spirit but neglect the Word out of which he teaches. The only safeguard against lies is to have remaining within us both the Word that "we heard from the beginning" and the anointing that we received from him. It is by these old possessions, not by new teachings or teachers, that we shall remain in the truth.[68]

How are you doing in your combined disciplines of "honoring the Word" and "honoring the Spirit"? _____

RESPOND—*What Will You Do with What You Know?*

(1) During the next two weeks, try out the eight methods of Bible study outlined in this unit.

THE SIGNIFICANCE OF THE BIBLE
UNIT 3

Organize your study this way: Spend the first week on method #1 reading and re-reading one book of the Bible. In week two, use a different one of the other seven methods of Bible study each day. You may eventually settle on a handful of methods you use most often, but you should be familiar with all eight.

(2) Start keeping a journal (or continue if you already keep one) of the spiritual impressions you gain in Bible study. It's been said that "the palest ink is better than the best retentive memory."

(3) Purchase for your library at least one of the five essential tools discussed in this unit as well as one of the additional resources. The list below includes a number of "tried and true" editions you may want to choose from (all of these resources are available for purchase at www.frankshivers.com).

REFERENCES AND COMMENTARIES

Cruden's Bible Dictionary
Halley's Handbook on the Bible
What the Bible is All About, Henrietta Mears
Nelson's Quick Reference (Chapter by Chapter Commentary), Warren Wiersbe
Young's Analytical Concordance
Vincent Word Studies of the New Testament
Matthew Henry's One Volume Commentary of the Bible
The Believer's Bible Commentary, William MacDonald
The Bible Knowledge Commentary, John F. Walvoord and Roy B. Zuck (Editors)
More Evidence that Demands a Verdict, Josh McDowell

DEVOTIONAL CLASSICS

Morning and Evening, C.H. Spurgeon
My Utmost for His Highest, Oswald Chambers
Streams in the Desert, L. B. Cowman

BIBLE STUDY WORKBOOKS

Following God Series, Wayne Barber, Eddie Rasnake, Richard Shephard. (AMG International)
Experiencing God, Henry Blackaby

SPIRITUAL CLASSICS

The Best of A.W. Tozer, Warren Wiersbe
Absolute Surrender, Andrew Murray
Abide in Christ, Andrew Murray
Spiritual Lessons, J. Oswald Sanders
The Practice of Godliness, Jerry Bridges

BIBLE TRANSLATION—GUIDE TO ABBREVIATIONS

The wide range of English Bible translations available today offers another opportunity for exploring Scripture in depth. Comparing different versions can provide helpful insights into word meanings, but the variety of options can be confusing. The list below identifies the names and abbreviations of a number of the more popular translations.

King James Version—KJV
New King James Version—NKJV
New International Version—NIV
English Standard Version—ESV
Holman Christian Standard Bible—HCSB
New Living Translation—NLT

Revised Standard Version—RSV
New Revised Standard Version—NRSV
New American Standard Bible—NASB
New Century Version—NCV
Contemporary English Version—CEV
Good News Translation/Today's English Version—GNT/TEV

NEGLECT NOT: SCRIPTURE

Search the scripture: for in them ye think ye have eternal life and they are they that testify of me.
—John 5:39

This word "search" means to investigate, to examine, and to find out something. It is an emphatic command of our Lord. Have you been obedient to this command to search the Scriptures, or are you guilty of neglect? Consider other biblical teachings about the importance of this discipline:

- For the Word of God is quick, and powerful, and sharper than a two-edged sword, piercing even to the dividing asunder of soul and spirit and of the joints and marrow, and is a discerner of the thoughts and intents of the heart.—Hebrews 4:12
- All scripture is given by inspiration of God and is profitable for doctrine, for reproof, for correction, for instruction in righteousness that the man of God may be perfect, thoroughly furnished unto all good works.—2 Timothy 3: 16-17

No Scripture is exhausted by a single explanation. The flowers of God's garden bloom not only double, but sevenfold; they are continually pouring forth fresh fragrance.[69]
—C. H. Spurgeon

In Uganda, the native Christians journey daily through high grass to a place of solitude to meet with God. It becomes apparent when someone fails to meet with God for a few days because grass grows up on this path. When this lack of discipline is noticed, concerned fellow believers comment, "Brother, there is grass growing up on your path."

How about you? Is there grass growing upon your path to solitude with God in His Word? Have you neglected Holy Scripture? Have you allowed pleasure or people to keep you from it? The Bereans "searched the scripture daily" (Acts 17:11), refusing to let grass grow upon their path to intimacy with the Almighty. Determine to be of the same mind, neglecting not the intake of daily mega-doses of Scripture.

UNIT 4

OVERVIEW OF THE BIBLE
"A handbook of salvation."

That's how John Stott describes The Holy Bible. And that, in a nutshell, is why studying to internalize its message is so critical, as we discussed in the previous unit. Stott further explains:

> The whole Bible unfolds the divine scheme of salvation—man's creation in God's image, his fall through disobedience into sin and under judgment, God's continuing love for him in spite of his rebellion, God's eternal plan to save him through his covenant of grace with a chosen people, culminating in Christ; the coming of Christ as the Savior, who died to bear man's sin, was raised from death, was exalted to heaven and sent the Holy Spirit; and man's rescue first from guilt and alienation, then from bondage, and finally from mortality in his progressive experience of the liberty of God's children.[70]

To fully appreciate how we have this remarkable message preserved in writing, though, it is important to explore the background of this amazing book.

TWO PARTS, ONE WHOLE

Our word "Bible" comes from the Latin *biblia*, meaning "books." The term is fitting because the Bible is a compilation of smaller books that recounts God's acts and communication with man. It consists of 66 books divided into two divisions: the Old Testament and the New Testament.

> *The sole criterion of the canon (straightedge, ruler, or measuring rod) of Scripture is inspiration (2 Timothy 3:16-17), God's testimony through the Holy Spirit.*[71]
>
> —Paige Patterson

The word "testament" can also be rendered "covenant"—in this case, an agreement or promise between God and man. The Old Testament is God's covenant with man regarding salvation prior to Christ's coming. Before Jesus' earthly life, the Old Testament was the only body of Holy Scripture. There was no New Testament.

The New Testament is God's covenant with man about salvation in Christ Jesus, and it provides significant contrasts with the Old Testament. The old covenant focuses on Mt. Sinai (the Law); the new covenant centers on Mt. Calvary (grace). The Old Testament records preparations for the coming of Jesus; the New Testament recounts His arrival, life, works, death, burial, and resurrection for the redemption of mankind.

WORD WISDOM: GRACE

The unmerited favor of God—clemency, kindness—toward man in salvation, demonstrated through His Son Jesus Christ at Calvary (*Ephesians 2:8-9*). An acrostic of Grace describes Grace as God's Riches At Christ's Expense. Grace is not confined to salvation because it also makes possible ongoing forgiveness and change in the believer's life by the power of God.

GROWING IN KNOWLEDGE, LIVING BY FAITH
UNIT 4

REVIEW

(1) What are some of the elements John Stott says make up the "handbook of salvation"? _____

(2) Explain why "Bible" is an appropriate word for the Christian Scriptures. _____

(3) Another word for "testament" is _____.

(4) Why are the two major divisions of Scripture called "Old Testament" and "New Testament"? _____

(5) What are the two primary contrasts between the Old and New Testaments? _____

THE IN'S AND OUT'S OF SCRIPTURE

If certain writings have been chosen to be included in Scripture, a reasonable question arises: What was the criterion for the inclusion (canonicity) of the 66 books in the Bible and the exclusion of others?

Pastor and theologian Philip Comfort provides an excellent summary of how the various writings were accepted into the Bible:

> Whether we think of the prophets of Old Testament times or the apostles and their God-given associates of the New, the recognition at the very time of their writing that they were authentic spokesmen for God is what determines the intrinsic canonicity of their writing. It is altogether God's Word only if it is God-breathed. We can be assured that the books under question were received by the church of the apostolic age precisely when they had been certified by an apostle as being thus inspired.[72]

> "Canonical" describes the ancient writings—both before and after the time of Christ—that have been accepted by Christians as being divinely inspired and therefore, included in the Bible.

Under God's leadership, selection was based upon a book's being divinely inspired. Books written by apostles under the inspiration of the Holy Spirit were accepted into the New Testament, and those written by prophets into the Old Testament. That the writings were produced by divine inspiration is the key. All others were rejected.

> *And in every case the principle on which a book was accepted, or doubts against it laid aside, was the historical tradition of apostolicity.*[73]
>
> —B. B. Warfield

The report on the Bible issued by the Lambeth Conference in 1958 in part stated: "the Church is 'not Over' the Holy Scriptures, but 'under' them, in the sense that the process on cannonization was not one whereby the Church conferred authority on the books but one whereby the Church acknowledged them to possess authority."

—The Lambeth Conference 1958
(SPCK, 1958, Part 2, Page 5)

Nothing is in the Bible that shouldn't be, and nothing is missing that ought to be. Believe it against the opinion of any scientist, teacher, preacher, or friend. It is the Word of Him who cannot lie. As D. L. Moody affirms:

> When Christ said, "The Scriptures cannot be broken" He meant every word He said. Devil and man and hell have been in league for centuries to try to break the Word of God, but they cannot do it. If you get it for your footing, you have a good footing, for time and eternity. "Heaven and earth shall pass away, but my Word shall not pass away." My friends, that Word is going to live, and there is no power in perdition or in earth to blot it out.[74]

There is no saving power in the words of men. The devil does not relinquish his grasp upon his prisoners at the bidding of mere mortals. No word has authority for him but the Word of God.[75]

—John Stott

The divine inspiration of Scripture means that the Bible is fully alive. It is life-giving communication from God to man, bearing the power to convict man of sin and draw him to God. No other book in the world can do that.

W. A. CRISWELL SERMON ON CANONIZATION OF SCRIPTURE
(excerpt)

In the early church, false writings were being distributed that clearly were not divinely inspired of God as claimed because they "preached another Jesus" (2 Corinthians 11:4) or consisted of fabricated content. These books were rejected from inclusion in the Bible. There were those who cried in their dogmatism saying, "We must add books to the Old Testament canon, to those thirty-nine. We must add books to them." And in the Council of Trent and in the Synod of Jerusalem and in the Council of the bishops of Hippo, they said, "We must add to those thirty-nine books the Apocrypha." So they added them, but God said, "Not so, take them out and away." And there's not a fair-minded Jew in the earth today, nor a fair-minded Christian, who would add the monstrous absurdities of the Apocrypha to this holy revelation. God says "No." And when I hold the Book in my hand, you won't find an Apocrypha in it. And there were those who said, "We must add to the twenty-seven books of the New Testament. We must add other gospels. And we must add other epistles. And we must add other apocalypses." So they wrote gospels and epistles and apocalypses in proliferation. But God said, "No." And in the Book that I hold in my hand, there are twenty-seven books in the New Testament as it has been from the first Christian centuries, and none are to be added and none are to be taken away. And to add those apocrypha, and apocalypses, and epistles, and gospels is like tying fruit to a tree. It withers and rots and fades away. So it is with God's Word. God's Word was forever fixed in heaven. And the copy I have of it in this earth is according to the mandate and authority of Almighty God. "The grass withereth, the flower fadeth, but the Word of God shall stand forever."[76]

GROWING IN KNOWLEDGE, LIVING BY FAITH
UNIT 4

REVIEW

(1) What does "canonical" mean?_____
(2) The key to a book's inclusion in the Bible is _____
(3) The Old Testament was written by men who were _____, the New Testament by those who were _____.
(4) How many books are there in the Bible? ____.
  Of those ____ are in the Old Testament, _____ are in the New Testament.

PUTTING THE PIECES TOGETHER

The Old and New Testaments affirm each other. The Old Testament is recognized as the old covenant by the Apostle Paul in the New Testament scripture, 2 Corinthians 3:14. The New Testament declares God's will for mankind in His Son Jesus Christ and offers the new covenant of grace, as promised in the Old Testament and affirmed in the New (Jeremiah 31:31-34; 1 Corinthians 11:25; 2 Corinthians 3:6; Hebrews 8:8-13; 9:15; 12:24).

THE OLD TESTAMENT

The 39 books of the Old Testament are divided into five categories:

(1) Pentateuch—Genesis, Exodus, Leviticus, Numbers, Deuteronomy;
(2) Historical Books—Joshua, Judges, Ruth, 1 & 2 Samuel, 1 & 2 Kings, 1 & 2 Chronicles, Ezra, Nehemiah, Esther;
(3) Poetic—Job, Psalms, Proverbs, Ecclesiastes, Song of Solomon;
(4) Prophetic (two categories)
  (a) Major Prophets—Isaiah, Jeremiah, Lamentations, Ezekiel, Daniel;
  (b) Minor Prophets—Hosea, Joel, Amos, Obadiah, Jonah, Micah, Nahum, Habakkuk, Zephaniah, Haggai, Zechariah, Malachi.

> **WORD WISDOM: MERCY**
>
> (1) The compassion, lovingkindness, pity and goodness expressed by God for sinners and their plight of condemnation (*Ephesians 2:4; Romans 11:30-32*).
> (2) The pity, compassion, and love of God expressed to believers in times of spiritual failure (*Psalm 51:1; 103:8-11*).
> (3) Christians are to exhibit mercy to those who sin and repent (*Matthew 5:8*). C. H. Spurgeon exhorts, "Mercies should be remembered. It is a great wrong to God when we bury his mercies in the grave of unthankfulness."[77]

THE NEW TESTAMENT

The New Testament consists of 27 books, also divided into five categories:

(1) The Gospels—Matthew, Mark, Luke, John;
(2) History—Acts of the Apostles;
(3) The Pauline Epistles—Romans, 1 & 2 Corinthians, Galatians, Ephesians, Philippians, Colossians, 1 & 2 Thessalonians, 1 & 2 Timothy, Titus, Philemon;
(4) The General Epistles—Hebrews, James, 1 & 2 Peter, 1, 2 & 3 John, Jude;
(5) Book on Last Things—Revelation.

OVERVIEW OF THE BIBLE
UNIT 4

REVIEW

(1) How do the Old and New Testaments affirm each other? _____

(2) What are the five categories of books in the Old Testament? _____

(3) What books are classified as "poetic?" _____
(4) What books are classified as "prophetic?" _____
(5) What are the five categories of books in the New Testament? _____

(6) Name the "Pauline epistles." _____
(7) What is the book of "last things?" _____

A SYNOPSIS OF BOOKS IN THE BIBLE

Each book in the Bible—whether Old or New Testament—makes a unique contribution to telling the story of God's revelation of Himself to people.

OLD TESTAMENT

Genesis. Creation; the flood of Judgment; Israel's enslavement.

Exodus. Plagues; Moses leads Israelites out of captivity; Ten Commandments; Blueprints for the Tabernacle.

Leviticus. The ceremonial law and the revelation of Christ in the law.

Numbers. 40-year wilderness wanderings begin; murmurings of the Israelites.

Deuteronomy. The law rehearsed; the death of Moses.

Joshua. The minority report to trust God to enter the Promised Land and possess it.

Judges. A time of "no king" but of 13 Judges. Judges 2:16-19 summarizes Israel's history at this time.

Ruth. The story of Naomi, Ruth and Boaz.

1 & 2 Samuel. Story of the reigns of Saul and David; Narrative of David's adultery and murder of Uriah the Hittite.

1 & 2 Kings. Record of the reign of the Jewish Kings who ruled Israel. What began as one nation eventually divided into two.

1 & 2 Chronicles. Record of the kings and genealogy with encouragement to rebuild the temple.

Ezra. The story of the return of the Jews from the Babylonian captivity.

Nehemiah. Nehemiah's leadership in the rebuilding of the walls about Jerusalem and reinstitution of worship despite grave opposition. A time of revival.

Esther. Queen Esther intervenes on behalf of the Jews and saves them from a holocaust.

Job. Satan tempts a righteous and godly man in Edom without success. A narrative of one man's patience, endurance, and faith despite suffering and calamity. Psalms. The hymnbook of the Bible, comprised mostly of David's songs of praise and adoration to God for His many deliverances and provisions.

Proverbs. Wise instructions on living ethically, morally, and spiritually.

GROWING IN KNOWLEDGE, LIVING BY FAITH

UNIT 4

Ecclesiastes. An empty man's search for meaning and significance.
Song of Solomon. A love song between Christ and His Church.
Isaiah. Prophecy of Christ 700 years before His coming; proclamation of God's judgment on Judah.
Jeremiah. The "weeping prophet."
Lamentations. Jeremiah's sorrow over Israel's calamity.
Ezekiel. God's glory and the honor of His name.
Daniel. Story of Daniel, the man who would not bow to compromise; major prophecies concerning Christ.
Hosea. The marriage of Hosea and Gomer illustrates the redeeming love of God for a wayward people.
Joel. A call to repentance. Uses the imagery of locusts regarding judgment.
Amos. Pronouncement of judgment upon Israel, rejection of God's warning.
Obadiah. Announcement of the doom of Edom.
Jonah. The story of Jonah, the fugitive fleeing from God who finally becomes the first foreign missionary; revival in Nineveh and the city is spared judgment.
Micah. God expects man to "to do justly, and to love mercy" and live obediently; prophesies the birthplace of the Son of God.
Nahum. Proclaims the destruction of Nineveh (125 years after Jonah).
Habakkuk. The victory of faith over difficulty; "The just shall live by faith."
Zephaniah. Preaching of judgment in the midst of a false revival.
Haggai. The House of God sat uncompleted; Haggai's bold preaching got the people back to work on it.
Zechariah. The re-building of the temple; messianic prophecies.
Malachi. The backsliding of Israel and the priests; a bold pronouncement against it.

> **WORD WISDOM: FAITH**
>
> To exhibit trust in and reliance upon God and all He says (*Hebrews 11:1, 6; Ephesians 2:8-9*). According to Martin Luther, "Faith is a living and unshakable confidence, a belief in God so assured that a man would die a thousand deaths for its sake."[78] Trust is believing Jesus *can*; Faith is believing Jesus *will*.

NEW TESTAMENT

Gospel of Matthew. Jesus is presented as Teacher and the promised Messiah of the Old Testament; genealogy of Jesus through Joseph.
Gospel of Mark. Life and works of Jesus the Messiah; pictures Jesus as a servant; roughly a third of Mark recounts the last week of Jesus' life.
Gospel of Luke. The compassionate Christ, the Savior of all; genealogy of Jesus through Mary; largest of the gospels.
Gospel of John. Presents the person and work of Christ as the Son of God and His acts and discourses not recorded elsewhere; the "salvation textbook."
The Acts of the Apostles. Acts of the Holy Spirit through early church evangelism; the story of how the Gospel spread throughout the world; Paul's missionary journeys.
Epistle (letter) to the Romans. Doctrine of salvation (justification by faith), coupled with duties of the Christian life.
First Epistle to the Corinthians. A letter of correction and direction to a "troubled church"; abuse of the Lord's Supper and the matter of lawsuits.

OVERVIEW OF THE BIBLE

UNIT 4

Second Epistle to the Corinthians. Help for a "troubled church," part 2; Paul gives defense of his authority as an apostle.

Epistle to the Galatians. Christian liberty; freedom by God's grace; repudiation of legalism.

Epistle to the Ephesians. Christian living; the believer's position in Christ Jesus.

Epistle to the Philippians. The Christian's joy and message.

Epistle to the Colossians. A letter of rebuke regarding false teaching in the church at Colossae; the apostle Paul writes to establish saints soundly in the Truth.

First Epistle to the Thessalonians. Last Things (Second Coming of Christ) and teaching on purity.

Second Epistle to the Thessalonians. Last Things; the Apostle Paul corrects an error regarding the coming of the Lord.

First Epistle to Timothy. Ministerial instruction to pastors and how all should conduct themselves in the church; requirements for being a deacon.

Second Epistle to Timothy. The Apostle Paul's last words to Timothy; final instruction, warning and encouragement to his "son in the faith."

Epistle to Titus. The Apostle Paul instructs the pastor Titus; people are to practice what they profess.

Epistle to Philemon. A moving narrative of a runaway slave who, after coming to salvation, returns to his legal owner, also a Christian; "for love's sake"; example of forgiveness.

Epistle to the Hebrews. Christ "above all"; "better than" the angels, prophets, the Levitical priests, etc.

Epistle of James. "Faith without works is dead"; live like a believer.

First Epistle of Peter. Encouraging words to suffering saints; mentions baptism.

Second Peter. Warning about false doctrine; insights about the Lord's return.

First Epistle of John. Birthmarks of the true believer; the conduct of a child of God.

Second Epistle of John. Stay loyal to the truth of God; always walk in the love of God.

Third Epistle of John. No person should be like Diotrephes who loves to have pre-eminence in the church; the saints should serve together in love.

Epistle of Jude. Warnings of false teachers; an appeal for the saints to contend earnestly for the faith.

The Revelation. Commendation and condemnation of the seven churches; the future of the church revealed; Christ's ultimate conquest.

REVIEW

(1) In which book of the Old Testament is the Ten Commandments first recorded? _____

(2) Which six books tell the story of the kings of Israel? _____
_____

(3) Which book is the "hymnbook of the Bible"? _____

(4) Who was the "weeping prophet"? _____

(5) What New Testament book is considered "the salvation textbook?" _____

(6) Which four New Testament books tell the story of Christ's life on earth? _____
_____

(7) Which book tells the history of the early church? _____

GROWING IN KNOWLEDGE, LIVING BY FAITH

UNIT 4

(8) In which book is the Doctrine of Salvation spelled out most completely? _____

(9) Name the New Testament book that focuses on Christian liberty: _____

(10) What book would you go to in order to read the story of a runaway slave who became a Christian? _____

(11) Which book reminds us that "faith without works is dead"? _____

REFLECT—Consider What This Means

(1) Francis Dixon of the Landsdowne Bible School and Postal Fellowship wrote: "There is not one single proved inaccuracy in the whole Bible. The Bible is accurate historically, geographically, genealogically, scientifically, psychologically, typologically, and verbally."[79] Even if there were no "external" verification of Scripture, why is Dixon's contention legitimate? _____

(2) John Paton, missionary for the South Sea islanders, translated the Scriptures but hit a brick wall trying to come up with a word to convey the concept of faith, trust, or believing. Then one day a native ran into Paton's study, flopped from exhaustion, and exclaimed, "It feels so good to rest my whole weight in this chair." Paton had his translation: "Faith is resting your whole weight on God." How fully do you rest your whole weight on God?[80]

(3) A well-known children's song declares: "The B – I – B – L – E, yes that's the Book for me. I stand alone on the Word of God. The B – I – B – L – E." In what ways do you "stand alone on the Word of God"? _____

RESPOND—What Will You Do with What You Know?

(1) During your Bible study time in the next 30 days, read through the introductions to each book of the Bible in whichever study Bible, commentary, or Bible handbook you began using in Unit 3. Note in your journal new insights or background you discover from your reading.

(2) Choose a friend or family member to whom you can explain the requirement for canonicity as well as the general outline of the Bible.

(3) Read *What the Bible Is All About*, the time-tested classic overview of Scripture by Henrietta Mears.

UNIT 5

PRAYER, FASTING, AND SOLITUDE

The core spiritual disciplines of prayer, fasting, and solitude have been practiced by serious Christians for centuries. Each has its well-defined place in the spiritual growth and sanctification of the believer. In Unit 1, we discussed the "have been saved," "am being saved," and "will be saved" aspects of salvation. In this unit, we explore how the Holy Spirit works through the believer's prayer, fasting, and solitude to work out the "am being saved" salvation "here and now." You'll find guidelines to help you incorporate each of these practices into your life with God.

WORD WISDOM: SANCTIFICATION

To appoint or set apart for a holy or special purpose (*1 Corinthians 1:2; Hebrews 10:10*). Believers are divinely "set apart" at conversion and enabled to progress in sanctification by the power of God (*1 Peter 1:15-16; 2 Chronicles 29:5; Proverbs 4:18; 2 Corinthians 7:1*). Spurgeon explains, "Sanctification is the work of God's Spirit (*2 Thessalonians 2:13*), whereby we are renewed in the whole man after the image of God (*Ephesians 4:24*), and are enabled more and more to die to sin, and live to righteousness (*Romans 6:11*)."[81]

Ray C. Stedman defines sanctification as:

> the process by which the inner worth which God imparts to our human spirit by faith in Christ begins to work itself out into our conduct. We actually begin to change. We begin to be like what we actually are. Therefore, our attitudes change, and our actions change, and our habits begin to change, and we stop certain things and begin others. Our whole demeanor is different; we become much more gracious, happy, wholesome persons.[82]

The first thought and the first word of the day belong to God.[83]
—Dietrich Bonhoeffer

Let's move from theology to knee-ology! Power for victory in spiritual warfare is found in prayer.[84]
—Robert R. Lawrence

PRAYER

The simple truth about prayer is this: Prayer is talking to God. You can talk to God just as surely as you can talk with any other person you know. The less simple reality, though, seems to be that many Christians—perhaps you among them—have some tough times with that simple truth. But so much is to be gained through effective prayer that the time you invest in growing your prayer life will pay tremendous dividends in spiritual development.

The Bible is a letter God has sent to us; prayer is a letter we send to Him.[85]

—Matthew Henry

Prayer is to the believer's victory over sin and fellowship with God what oxygen is to our lungs. It is absolutely vital. The discipline of prayer at the start of the day and throughout the day is essential to growth. Prayer leads to the four P's of spirituality:

- Presence of God,
- Power of God,
- Product of God,
- Plan of God.

> *I ought to spend the best hours in communion with God. It is my noblest and most fruitful employment and is not to be thrust into the corner.*[86]
>
> —Robert Murray M'Cheyne

A. W. Tozer recognized not only the difficulty but the reward of a strong prayer life:

> It is well that we accept the hard truth now: The man who would know God must give time to Him. He must count no time wasted that is spent in the cultivation of His acquaintance. He must give himself to meditation and prayer hours on end. So did the saints of old, the glorious company of the apostles, the Godly fellowship of the prophets and the believing members of the holy church in all generations. And so must we if we would follow in their train.[87]

So the task we all face is how to make the most of our prayer time.

> *Hurried devotion makes weak faith, feeble convictions, questionable piety. To be little with God is to do little for God.*[88]
>
> —E. M. Bounds

HOW TO PRAY

Prayer entails "asking" God (Matthew 7:8), and "asking" works because it's the authorized and anointed means given to Christians by God to have needs met personally and for others corporately (Matthew 7:7-8). Asking works because God promises it will: "Call unto me, and I will answer thee, and shew thee great and mighty things, which thou knowest not" (Jeremiah 33:3). Christians are to trust the promise of God about prayer and exhibit faith in His ability and power to answer in accordance with His divine will and good pleasure (James 1:6; Luke 22:42).

Spurgeon points out that sometimes words are not even necessary in the asking:

> For real business at the mercy seat give me a home-made prayer, a prayer that comes out of the depths of your heart, not because you invented it, but because the Holy Spirit put it there. Though your words are broken and your sentences disconnected God will hear you. Perhaps you can pray better without words than with them. There are prayers that break the back of words; they are too heavy for any human language to carry.[89]

PRAYER, FASTING, AND SOLITUDE
UNIT 5

However you choose to pray, though, answers will come. According to John Bisagno:

> Answered prayer is not a miracle, it is a law. It will always be, when the laws are kept and certain rules are observed. It is always to be expected! When the child of God prays and his prayers are answered, three things have happened: he has prayed in faith believing, he has prayed specifically and has thereby met the conditions of a loving Heavenly Father, and the Father has responded.[90]

> *I would sooner see you eloquent with God than with men.*[91]
> —C. H. Spurgeon

REVIEW

(1) What are the four P's of spirituality? _____

(2) According to A. W. Tozer, what do you have to give God in order to get to know Him?
_____

(3) John Bisagno says that answered prayer is a _____.

PRAYING THE MODEL PRAYER

In Matthew 6:9-13, the Lord provides a model prayer. Theologian Jon Courson explains how Jesus' model prayer offers encouragement to the believer:

> I can't hit like Babe Ruth, paint like Michelangelo, or sing like George Beverly Shea. But you know what? I can pray like John Knox, like Martin Luther, and like Charles Spurgeon, because I can pray the same prayer they prayed. It is the perfect prayer because it came from the perfect Pray-er: Jesus Christ. You can pray this prayer daily, hourly, whenever you like. And you will find yourself in incredible company with the great saints of the ages, with believers of all other flavors, who all love God and address Him as Father because of their relationship to the Son.[92]

Jesus' prayer is not intended to be prayed only verbatim. It also serves as a pattern for our own prayers. The outline below shows how.

1. God's Pardon to be remembered—"Our Father who art in Heaven."
Implied by the word "our" is the story of man's redemption from Satan and sin unto God. Only the "born again," due to their adoption into His family as sons and daughters, have the privilege and honor to address God in this personal manner (Galatians 4:4-7; Romans 8:14-15). Express gratitude to God for making this possible and for granting access to His throne 24/7.

> *It is far better to begin with God—to see His face first, to get my soul near Him before it is near another.*[93]
> —Robert Murray M'Cheyne

GROWING IN KNOWLEDGE, LIVING BY FAITH
UNIT 5

2. God's Person to be reverenced—"Hallowed be Thy name."
You are to pray that God's name—it speaks of who God is and His holiness, love, power, authority—will be treated with respect and reverence.

3. God's Program to be expanded—"Thy kingdom come." You are to pray that God's rule will encompass the whole world. Pray that there will be less and less sin and more and more people who love Jesus. Wouldn't it really be great if everybody loved Jesus and lived for Him? You are to pray for that to be true. Pray for friends and others to be saved. As part of your daily routine, pray: "Lord help me do my part in fulfilling the Great Commission today that your Kingdom will come sooner rather than later."

4. God's Plan to be accomplished—"Thy will be done." You are to pray that what God wants to do in, with, and through your life will be done without hindrance or delay, just as it is done among the host of heaven. To pray in this manner, lay aside personal wants and desires and be completely open to His plan for your life, a plan that may include full-time Christian service. You are to pray that His plans also will be fulfilled in Christians, the church, and nations.

> **MODUS OPERANDI OF PRAYER**
> A rescue rope is thrown from the shore to a drowning man, and he is pulled to safety. Note the shore is not pulled to the man but the man to the shore. This is how prayer operates. In praying (pulling the rope of dialog with God), a person is pulled to God's perspective and plan, not God to man's. Prayer changes *us*, not God.

5. God's Provision to be given—"Give us this day our daily bread."
Pray that God will give you everything needed. In sickness, ask Him to give health, in times of loneliness to give a friend, in times of hunger to give food, and in times of sorrow to give comfort. There is no need to worry about tomorrow since God is as much in control of it as He is of today. Just ask Him to help, and He will. Of this phrase in the Lord's prayer, Andrew Murray says, "When the child (Christian) has yielded himself to the Father in the care for His name, His Kingdom and His will, he has full liberty to ask for his daily bread."[94]

6. God's Pardon to be known—"Forgive us our debts (sins) as we forgive our debtors."
In the same measure believers forgive when wronged, they are to pray God will forgive them. And in the same manner God forgives the believer (i.e., without deserving it), the believer is to forgive those who do him wrong. Fellowship with, not relationship to God, demands that believers forgive others. Confession and repentance of sin is necessary every day, so keep short accounts of sin. Don't save spiritual soiled garments until "wash day." Wash 'em daily! (1 John 1:7–9)

> *When people fail, don't rub it in. Rub it out. Forgive them.*[95]
> —Jon Courson

7. God's Prevention to be experienced—"And lead us not into temptation."
Pray that God will not only protect from sin but also from the temptation that causes it

and from walking into its arena. If you're not tempted to do wrong, chances are you won't. At the dawn of each new day, the believer should pray, "O Lord keep me from temptation today and especially the one that doth so easily beset me" (Hebrews 12:1).

8. God's Protection to be demonstrated—"But deliver me from the evil one." Pray that God will not allow Satan to harm or injure your spiritual walk. This is possible because "greater is He that is in me than he that is in the world" (1 John 4:4). God gives the power and strength to defeat Satan.

9. God's Praise to be exhibited—"For thine is the Kingdom, the power and the glory forever. Amen." The model prayer ends with a doxology of praise. Praise is giving God the honor due Him. Close your prayers by telling God how much you love, honor, and revere Him. John Calvin said of this doxology that it "not only warms our hearts to press toward the glory of God…but also to tell us that all our prayers…have no other foundation than God alone."[96]

PRAY USING "ACTS"

An acrostic of the word ACTS provides a helpful checklist for the items you will want to pray regularly. Base your prayer in this sequential order:

- A = Adoration (praise and worship of God);
- C = Confession (repentance and cleansing);
- T = Thanksgiving (gratitude for salvation, daily provision, and protection);
- S = Supplication (petitioning God as in Matthew 7:7).

> *Ask, and it shall be given you; seek, and ye shall find; knock, and it shall be opened unto you.*
> —Matthew 7:7

HOW TO END A PRAYER?

Prayer in Jesus' name certainly is taught in John 14:13-14. However, simply attaching "In Jesus name" at the end of prayer holds no magic power. Praying in Jesus' name means to pray in His authority with full confidence that God will hear and answer petitions asked in His name that are in agreement with His divine will (*1 John 5:14-15*).

PRAY THE SCRIPTURES AND MEDITATIONS

There is no greater praying than praying Scripture. The Psalms in particular can be easily adapted and turned into personal prayers. As you read through the Bible, you'll also discover other prayers you may want to make your own.

In his commentary on David's prayer in Psalm 5:1-3, Matthew Henry explains the meditative aspect of praying:

> David's prayers were not his words only, but his mediations; as mediation is the best preparative for prayer, so prayer is the best issue of meditation. Meditation and prayer should go together.[97]

GROWING IN KNOWLEDGE, LIVING BY FAITH

UNIT 5

PRAY THE PRAYERS OF SAINTS AND HYMNS

The Valley of Vision, a collection of prayers of the saints, is a tremendous aid to the believer in jump-starting personal prayers. Great hymns of the faith can similarly be personalized and turned upward to God in praise and prayer. While prayers "borrowed" from saints and hymns do not substitute for personal praying, they can serve as a springboard to praying heartfelt and passionate prayers.

In 1695, Thomas Ken formatted a launchpad for prayer at the start of the day by declaring to God:

> Direct, control, suggest, this day,
> All I design, or do, or say
> That all my powers, with all their might,
> In Thy sole glory may unite.[98]

REGULAR PRAYER TIMES

The prophet Daniel prayed at set times and in a set place (Daniel 6:10). Make an appointment to meet God in prayer, scheduling the time and place each day. This is your "closet" prayer time. Plan the day around prayer, not prayer around the day. A regular prayer time will set you up for ongoing daily praying as Christians are told to "Pray continuously" (1 Thessalonians 5:18; Ephesians 6:18). Prayer works, so work hard at prayer.

REVIEW

(1) The prayer Jesus taught in Matthew 6:9-13 can be used in what two ways? _____
_____
(2) What is the significance of praying "Our Father"? _____
(3) What are the eight petitions of the Lord's Prayer? _____
_____
(4) What does the prayer acrostic ACTS stand for?
    A = _____
    C = _____
    T = _____
    S = _____
(5) How can psalms, hymns, and prayers of saints be used? _____
_____

INTERCESSORY PRAYER

> *The ultimate purpose of prayer isn't to change God, it is to change us.*[99]
>
> —D. A. Carson

PRAYER, FASTING, AND SOLITUDE
UNIT 5

It is a great privilege to pray for the concerns and needs of others—to intercede before God on their behalf. Journaling your prayer requests is a particularly valuable aid to powerful intercessory prayer. A weekly pattern like the one suggested below may help you focus on the intercessory needs of the people you know.

- Monday—"M" pray for Ministers and Missionaries;
- Tuesday—"T" for Troubled people who are experiencing trials and tribulation;
- Wednesday—"W" for Workers with governing authority in the political arena;
- Thursday—"T" for personal Tasks God has assigned you;
- Friday—"F" for Friends and Foes;
- Saturday—"S" for Sinners who need salvation and Saints who need revival;
- Sunday—"S" for the Service of the church and those who preach, sing and teach.

> *The real business of your life as a saved soul is intercessory prayer.*[100]
> —Oswald Chambers

> *Our first prayer was a prayer for ourselves; we asked that God would have mercy upon us, and blot out our sin.*[101]
> —C. H. Spurgeon

REVIEW

(1) Intercessory prayer focuses primarily on _____ instead of _____.
(2) List some of the categories of people you might want to remember to pray for each week. _____
_____
_____

FASTING

> *Fasting helps to express, to deepen, and to confirm the resolution that we are ready to sacrifice anything, to sacrifice ourselves to attain what we seek for the kingdom of God.*[102]
> —Andrew Murray

Fasting is abstinence from food, amusements, relationships, or television for the purpose of focusing more totally on God. Christians do not fast and pray to change the mind of God but to give God the chance to change their minds. They fast to exhibit a state of mind to do what they are not naturally inclined to do—to cut loose the instinctive impulsiveness of the flesh (carnal nature). Jesus commends the discipline of fasting, giving instruction regarding the practice (Matthew 6:16-17).

Arthur Wallis explains that fasting raises the intensity of our prayers:

> Fasting is calculated to bring a note of urgency and importunity into our praying, and to give force to our pleading in the court of heaven. The man who prays with fasting is giving heaven notice that he is truly in earnest....Not only so, but he is expressing his earnestness in a divinely-appointed way. He is using a means that God has chosen to make his voice to be heard on high.[103]

Fasting combined with prayer and proper motive makes it acceptable unto the Lord.

Bill Bright similarly outlines the power fasting brings to a person's prayer life:

> Fasting is the most powerful spiritual discipline of all the Christian disciplines. Through fasting and prayer, the Holy Spirit can transform your life. Fasting and prayer can also work on a much grander scale. According to Scripture, personal experience and observation, I am convinced that when God's people fast with a proper Biblical motive—seeking God's face not His hand—with a broken, repentant, and contrite spirit, God will hear from heaven and heal our lives, our churches, our communities, our nation and world. Fasting and prayer can bring about revival—a change in the direction of our nation, the nations of earth and the fulfillment of the Great Commission.[104]

> **WORD WISDOM: CARNAL**
>
> A Christian who lives under the control of the "flesh" and its sensual appetites instead of in the fullness of the Holy Spirit—a worldly Christian (*Romans 8:5-7; 1 Corinthians 3:1-4*).

Isaiah makes plain the objective of the spiritual fast: "Is this not the purpose of the fast I have chosen? To loosen the bands of wickedness, to undo heavy burdens, and to let the oppressed go free, and that ye break every yoke?" (Isaiah 58:6)

Scripture delineates a variety of reasons why believers engage in a spiritual fast:

- To bring the body into subjection to the Spirit (1 Corinthians 9:27);
- To prevail with God (Ezra 8:23; Mark 9:29);
- To liberate from the "yoke" of a sin's mastery (Isaiah 58:6b);
- To give added strength in temptation (Matthew 4:1-11);
- To give guidance in decision making (Nehemiah 1:4);
- To express mourning and repentance for personal or corporate sin (Ezra 9:5; Joel 2:12-13);
- To give strength to follow through victoriously with Holy Spirit-led decisions (Esther 4:16);
- To reveal God's plan for life (Acts 10:10);
- To intercede for another when he or she falls into sin (1 Kings 21:27);
- To drive Satan and the demons of hell back (Mark 9:17-29);
- To intercede for a personal enemy (Psalm 35:12-13);
- To humble the soul (Psalms 69:10; 1 Kings 21:27-29);
- To break the bondage of physical appetite (1 Corinthians 6:12-13);
- To express love and devotion to God (Luke 2:37).

PRAYER, FASTING, AND SOLITUDE
UNIT 5

No specific length of time for a fast is prescribed in Scripture. Rather, various durations—from part of a day to forty days—are described. The Lord does not impose a set timetable for the fast nor times for its observance but allows the Holy Spirit to direct the individual believer regarding both. Fasting is to be a personal and private matter, not engaged to gain the attention or admiration of man but solely the audience of God. Jesus is clear on this point:

> Moreover when ye fast, be not, as the hypocrites, of a sad countenance: for they disfigure their faces, that they may appear unto men to fast. Verily I say unto you, they have their reward. But thou, when thou fastest, anoint thine head, and wash thy face; That thou appear not unto men to fast, but unto thy Father which is in secret: and thy Father, which seeth in secret, shall reward thee openly. (Matthew 6:16-18)

The general question for the believer is not "should I fast?" but "when should I fast, for how long, and for what purpose?" However, where a person has problematic health issues, medical counsel may be necessary to determine what kind of fasting is appropriate.

REVIEW

(1) Christians fast in order to get God to change His mind about a matter. ❏ True ❏ False
(2) What are some of the reasons Bill Bright gives for calling fasting "the most powerful...of all the Christian disciplines"? _____
(3) This section notes fourteen reasons why believers fast. Without looking back, see if you can list at least five. Then review the entire list. _____
(4) What range of times is given as "acceptable" fasting periods in Scripture? _____
(5) Who is the only "audience" for a fast? _____

SOLITUDE

> *[Solitude is] a life-giving practice that enriches our hearts with the powerful gifts of clarity, cleansing, and strength.*[105]
> —Michael D. Warden

The practice of solitude is the withdrawal of oneself to a quiet, serene place in silence before the Lord. My preferred place of solitude is a local park in early morning where I am "shut up" with God to think, meditate, read, worship, and to pray inwardly. Solitude precedes my devotional time and together this is absolutely the best part of the day. Solitude may last a few minutes, several hours, or for days.

GROWING IN KNOWLEDGE, LIVING BY FAITH

UNIT 5

> *Why is it that some Christians, although they hear many sermons, make but slow advances in the divine life? Because they neglect their closets, and do not thoughtfully meditate on God's Word.*[106]
> —C. H. Spurgeon

Jesus practiced solitude (Luke 4:42), as did the prophet Elijah at Mount Horeb (1 Kings 19:11-13), and the Apostle Paul in Arabia (Galatians 1:17). Scripture reinforces the rewards of solitude:

- Be still and know that I am God (Psalm 46:10).
- Truly my soul silently waits for God; From Him comes my salvation. He only is my rock and my salvation; He is my defense; I shall not be greatly moved (Psalm 62:1-2, NKJV).
- My soul, wait silently for God alone, for my expectation is from Him (Psalm 62:5, NKJV).

> *"For those who make solitude a habit, the discipline becomes more than merely something you do. Solitude becomes a place you go—a sacred space set apart from the world and reserved for you and God alone....The practice of regular solitude with God changes us."*[107]
> —Michael D. Warden

In his book, *Waiting on God,* Andrew Murray offers extensive guidance on the discipline of solitude:

Let everyone who wants to learn the art of waiting on God remember the lesson: "Take heed, and be quiet." It is good that a man quietly wait. Take time to be separate from all friends and duties, all cares and joys; time to be still and quiet before God. Take time not only to secure stillness from man and the world, but from self and its energy. Let the Word and Prayer be very precious. But remember, even these may hinder the quiet waiting. The activity of the mind in studying the Word or giving expression to its thoughts in prayer, the activities of the heart, with its desires and hopes and fears, may so engage us that we do not come to the still waiting on the All-glorious One; our whole being is prostrate in silence before Him. Though at first, it may appear difficult to know how thus quietly to wait, with the activities of mind and heart for a time subdued, every effort after it will be rewarded. We will discover that it grows upon us, and the little season of silent worship will bring a peace and a rest that give a blessing not only in prayer, but all day.[108]

A. W. Tozer provides similar instruction:

Retire from the world each day to some private spot, even if it be only the bedroom (for a while I retreated to the furnace room for want of a better place). Stay in the secret place till the surrounding noises begin to fade out of your heart and a sense of God's presence envelops you....Listen for the inward Voice till you learn to recognize it. Listen to pray inwardly every moment. Call home your roving thoughts. Gaze on Christ with the eyes of your soul. Practice spiritual concentration.[109]

PRAYER, FASTING, AND SOLITUDE
UNIT 5

Solitude not only enriches the believer's walk with God but may lead to salvation for the unsaved. In his sermon "Solitude, Silence and Submission," Spurgeon explains how this happens:

> I commend solitude to any of you who are seeking salvation, first, that you may *study well your case as in the sight of God*. Few men truly know themselves as they really are. Therefore, I pray you, set apart some season every day, or at least some season as often as you can get it, in which the business of your mind shall be to take your longitude and latitude, that you may know exactly where you are. You may be drifting towards the rocks, and you may be wrecked before you know your danger. I implore you, do not let your ship go at full steam through a fog; but slacken speed a bit, and heave the lead, to see whether you are in deep waters or shallow. I am not asking you to do more than any kind and wise man would advise you to do; do I even ask you more than your own conscience tells you is right? Sit alone a while, that you may carefully consider your case.[110]

WORD WISDOM: HOLINESS

J. C. Ryle describes holiness as "the habit of being of one mind with God, according as we find His mind described in Scripture. It is the habit of agreeing in God's judgment; hating what He hates, loving what He loves, and measuring everything in this world by the standard of His Word. He who most entirely agrees with God, he is the most holy man." Holiness involves separation from all that contaminates and defiles (*Matthew 5:8; Romans 12:1; 1 Thessalonians 4:7; Hebrews 12:14*).[111]

REVIEW

(1) Name three people whom the Bible says practiced the discipline of solitude. _____

(2) "Be _____ and _____ that I am God." (Psalm 46:10)

(3) What are some of the "habits" J. C. Ryle says describe the nature of holiness? _____

(4) How does Spurgeon indicate that solitude can help bring a person to salvation? _____

NEGLECT NOT: SUPPLICATION

Men ought to always pray and not faint.
—Luke 18:1

When thou saith, "Seek my face," my heart said unto thee, "Thy face, Lord, will I seek."
—Psalm 27:8

Here's a one-line instruction on prayer:

Pray when you feel like it, when you don't feel like it, until you do feel like it.

Saints through the ages have offered a variety of encouragement in the importance of prayer and the need to pray specifically:

- Martin Lloyd Jones—"Always respond to every impulse to pray. The impulse to pray may come when you are reading or when you are battling with a text. I would make an absolute law of this—always obey such an impulse."[112]
- John Bunyan—"Pray often, for prayer is a shield to the soul, a sacrifice to God, and a scourge for Satan."[113]
- François Fénelon—"Of all the duties enjoined by Christianity none is more essential and yet more neglected than prayer."[114]
- C. H. Spurgeon—"There is a general kind of praying which fails for lack of precision. It is as if a regiment of soldiers should all fire off their guns anywhere. Possibly somebody would be killed, but the majority of the enemy would be missed."[115]
- David Jeremiah—"How often have we prayed something like, 'O Lord, be with cousin Billy now in a special way'? Have we stopped to consider what it is we're requesting? Imagine that you are a parent who is preparing to leave your children with a babysitter. Would you dream of saying, 'O, Betsy, I ask you now that you would be with my children in a special way?' No way. You would say, 'Betsy, the kids need to be in bed by 9 p.m. They can have one snack before their baths, and please make sure they finish their homework. You can reach us at this number if there's any problem. Any questions before we go?' We are very specific with our requests and instructions for our babysitters. We want them to know specifics. It should be no different with prayer."[116]
- Corrie Ten Boom—"When a Christian shuns fellowship with other Christians, the devil smiles. When he stops studying the Bible, the devil laughs. When he stops praying, the devil shouts for joy."[117]

So pray, pray, pray dear believer.

PRAYER, FASTING, AND SOLITUDE
UNIT 5

REFLECT—*Consider What This Means*

(1) C. J. Mahaney says that "The way we end today can clearly affect the way we encounter tomorrow."[118] In light of the spiritual disciplines of prayer, fasting, and solitude, how does the way you end each of your days affect your tomorrows? _____
_____

(2) Some things come into our lives that hinder the effectiveness of our prayers. Review the list of hindrances below, read the associated scriptures, and ask God to reveal any way in which your prayers are being hindered. Make notes of what God tells you.
  • Disobedience (Micah 3:4; Deuteronomy 1:43-45, Jeremiah 11:10f) _____
  _____
  • Arrogance (James 4:6-10; Job 35:12-13) _____
  _____
  • Hypocrisy (Mark 12:38-40; Matthew 15:1-9) _____
  _____
  • Refusal to help the poor (Proverbs 21:13) _____
  _____
  • Unconfessed sin (John 9:31; Isaiah 59:1-2; Psalm 66:18) _____
  _____
  • Unforgiving spirit (Mark 11:25) _____
  _____
  • Indifference toward the Word of God (Proverbs 28:9) _____
  _____
  • Wrong relationship with husband or wife (1 Peter 3:7) _____
  _____

(3) E. M. Bounds challenges:
  A desire for God that cannot break the chains of sleep is weak, able to do little for God after it has indulged itself fully. The desire for God that lags behind the Devil and the world at the beginning of the day will never catch up. The desire for God awoke the great saints of God and called them to communion with their Lord. Heeding and acting on this call gave their faith a grasp on God and gave to their hearts the sweetest and fullest revelation of God.[119]
  How are you doing in breaking "the chains of sleep" and making sure you're not playing "catch-up" with God each day? _____

RESPOND—*What Will You Do with What You Know?*

(1) J. Wilbur Chapman asks:
  Did you ever cultivate the habit of talking aloud to God? Sit down this very day and with up-turned face and open eyes talk to Him as to your father, as to the dearest friend you have, one to whom you can tell your most secret thoughts; tell them to Him. The very room where you sit will seem to be filled with angels; but best of all God will be there, for one could not long talk to Him without feeling Him to be near.[120]

For the next week, spend a few minutes each day doing as Chapman suggests—look up and pray out loud to God.

(2) Peter Lord's "2959 Plan" is an excellent prayer plan and journal that specifies a different category of people for which to pray daily. Consider getting a copy and using it as a guide for intercessory prayer.

(3) "Why do we grow so little? Why do we win so few? Why are we weak and powerless? Because we pray so little."[121] —John Bisagno. How little or much are you praying? Have you set a specific time and place each day for prayer and solitude? If not, decide now what your schedule and location will be. Keep to your schedule for the next 21 days (it takes 3 weeks to establish a new habit). Record here the time and place you have planned: _____
_____

(4) Sometime during the next week, decide on a time to fast, simply to seek God's face. It can be skipping one meal, a 12-hour fast, 2 days, or whatever you feel led (during any fast, DO NOT abstain from drinking water). If you're not accustomed to fasting, it's better to plan a short fast to which you can be faithful than a long one you can't manage. To make yourself accountable, note when and how long you plan to fast: _____
_____

(5) Select one book from the list below to read during the next month.
With Christ in the School of Prayer, Andrew Murray
The Practice of the Presence of God, Brother Lawrence
The Autobiography of George Mueller
Hudson Taylor's Spiritual Secret, Hudson Taylor
2959 Plan, Peter Lord (Park Avenue Baptist Church, Titusville, Florida)
Spiritual Disciplines of the Christian Life, Donald S. Whitney
Fast Your Way to Health, J. Harold Smith

(6) Right now, schedule a full day to spend in solitude with the Lord sometime during the next month. Plan a tranquil but safe place where you may spend uninterrupted time with God. Take your journal, books, Bible, hymnal, etc., but no other person. It is essential you go alone. This is a day set apart just for Jesus and you. Determine that you will respond only to phone calls that day that are *truly* an emergency.

UNIT 6

BAPTISM

My wedding band declares three things:
- That I love somebody—Mary, my wife;
- That I belong to somebody—Mary, my wife;
- That I submit to somebody—Mary, my wife.

Similarly, baptism states the same three things. It says to friends, family, and others:
- "I love somebody—Jesus Christ";
- "I belong to somebody—Jesus Christ";
- "I submit to somebody—Jesus Christ—to do all He asks."

Through baptism, the believer proclaims, "Now I belong to Jesus, and Jesus belongs to me—not just for the years of my time on earth but for all eternity." Baptism depicts what happened at the moment of salvation. As believers go under and come up from the water, baptism pictures how Jesus washed away their sins and gave a new life in Christ. To reflect this transformation, some "old-time preachers" had their converts enter the water on one side of the river and exit on the other side to symbolize the abandonment of the old life and the entrance into the new life in Christ.

> **WORD WISDOM: ADOPTION**
>
> Spiritual adoption is the divine decree that brings a sinner "sonship" in the family of God through new birth (*Romans 8:15*; *Galatians 4:5*). Though an outcast and enemy of God, a person is brought into God's family through the new birth and is given the full benefits and blessings—both presently and eternally—that belong to the Son, Jesus Christ (*1 John 3:1*). By adoption, we also receive the nature of Christ (*2 Corinthians 5:21*).

So as the wedding ring is a symbol of my marital union with Mary, baptism is a symbol of a believer's union with Christ. And note this: I am not married simply because I wear a wedding ring. A person may wear a ring and not be married. Just so, a person is not saved and does not becomes a Christian simply by being baptized, confirmed, or christened. It is possible to be baptized and not be a child of God, just like Simon Magus in Acts 8:13-23. Scripture is clear that before a person is baptized, he or she must be saved. Otherwise, the "statement" made by being baptized is a lie.

WHAT BAPTISM SAYS *FOR* THE SAINT

As soon as possible after becoming a Christian, a new believer should be baptized (Matthew 28: 18-20; Acts 2:38). Baptism is one of the two ordinances, or prescribed religious practices (the Lord's Supper is the other), that Jesus gave the church. In keeping with our wedding ring analogy, J. I. Packer notes that baptism is part of the Christian's identity:

> My baptism reminds me whose I am and whom I must serve; who it is that stands pledged to love and cherish me, and share with me eternally all that he has; and what love and loyalty I owe in return.[122]

GROWING IN KNOWLEDGE, LIVING BY FAITH

UNIT 6

Spurgeon likewise considers it a crucial part of knowing who we belong to:

> "Well," says one, "I do not think that I shall confess Christ; the dying thief did not confess him, did he? He was not baptized." No, but he was a dying thief, recollect; and if you are not baptized, I think that you will be a living thief; for you will rob God of his glory, you will rob his servant also of the comfort which he ought to receive.[123]

REVIEW

(1) Explain the analogy of a wedding ring to baptism. _____

(2) Just as putting on a wedding ring does not make a person married, being baptized does not make a person _____.

(3) Does baptism have power to cleanse of sin and to save? _____

(4) How soon after conversion should the new believer be baptized? _____

(5) According to J. I. Packer, what should baptism remind the believer of? _____

(6) What does spiritual adoption bring to the believer? _____

WHAT BAPTISM SAYS ABOUT THE SAVIOR

Baptism is a picture of what happened to Jesus during the time period from Good Friday through Easter morning:

- Lowering a person into the water tells how Jesus died on the cross for man's sin and was buried;
- Holding the person under water reflects that Jesus remained in the grave for three days;
- Raising the person out of the water mirrors Jesus' victorious resurrection.

Baptism's mode and meaning are bound together. The Greek word *baptizo* means "to immerse" in water. John the Baptist baptized converts "in" the Jordan River (Mark 1:5), and he is explicit in describing Jesus' baptism that He came up "out of the water" (Mark 1:10). The account of Philip's baptism of the eunuch states that they went down in the water and came up out of the water (Acts 8:38-39). Each of these baptisms clearly was by the mode of immersion. By being baptized this way, the believer pictures death to self, burial of sin, and resurrection to newness of life in Jesus Christ, and it testifies to the fact of Jesus' death, burial, and resurrection.

This symbolism can be depicted only through the New Testament mode of baptism by immersion. It is a marvelous lesson about what Jesus did before, on, and after the cross. He willingly allowed soldiers to place a crown of jagged thorns upon His head, hammer nails into His feet and hands, pluck hair from His face, compel Him to carry a cross to Calvary, and then pierce His side with a sword.

Jesus suffered so much because of His love for the world. While on the cross, He prayed, "Father forgive them for they know not what they do" (Luke 23:34), referring to all those responsible for

BAPTISM
UNIT 6

His crucifixion and manifesting nothing but love for His enemies. The body of Jesus was buried and sealed in the tomb of Joseph and guarded by Roman soldiers (Matthew 27:65). On the third day (Easter morning), the stone was rolled away by God, and Jesus was raised from the dead (Luke 24:6). For the next forty days, Jesus revealed Himself to many people before returning to heaven.

After His resurrection, Christ appeared to:

- Mary Magdalene (John 20:11-18);
- Other women (Matthew 28:9,10);
- Two disciples on Emmaus Road (Luke 24:13-35);
- Ten disciples (John 20:19-25);
- Thomas (John 20:26-31);
- Seven disciples on the Sea of Galilee (John 21:1-25);
- His disciples at the Great Commission (Matthew 28:16-20);
- The five hundred (1 Corinthians 15:6);
- Those at His ascension (Acts 1:9-10);
- Paul (Acts 9:3-6);
- John (Revelation 1:10-18).

Baptism says for Jesus, "I *am* he that liveth, and was dead; and, behold, I am alive for evermore, Amen; and have the keys of hell and of death" (Revelation 1:18). The church awaits His return.

WORD WISDOM: JUSTIFICATION

The act of God by which He wipes clean the slate of man's sin (He pardons us) and satisfies the claims of the Law through the saving work of His Son Jesus Christ. Justification for the believer means *just-as-if-I-never sinned* (Romans 4:25)—to be forgiven of all sin and completely acquitted of all offenses as if they had never occurred (Romans 8:1; Romans 5:1-11).

REVIEW

(1) What three phases of Jesus' experience between Good Friday and Easter morning are reflected by baptism? _____
(2) Where is there scriptural evidence that immersion is the only appropriate method of baptism? _____
(3) How does the act of baptism by immersion itself portray that it is the only correct means of baptism? _____
(4) From the list above, approximately how many people did the resurrected Christ appear to? _____
(5) Justification for the believer makes it just-_____ sinned.

GROWING IN KNOWLEDGE, LIVING BY FAITH
UNIT 6

WHAT BAPTISM SAYS TO THE SINNER

Baptism not only speaks for the saint and about the Savior, but it also speaks to the sinner. Baptism proclaims that Jesus loves the unsaved so much that He paid the ultimate price of death upon a cross for their salvation:

> For this *is* good and acceptable in the sight of God our Savior; who will have all men to be saved, and to come unto the knowledge of the truth. For *there* is one God, and one mediator between God and men, the man Christ Jesus; who gave himself a ransom for all, to be testified in due time. (1 Timothy 2:3-6)

> **WORD WISDOM: CONFESSION**
>
> (1) The acknowledgement of sin (*1 John 1:9; Ezra 10:11*). After he committed adultery, King David confessed his sin to God and pleaded for forgiveness and restoration (*Psalm 51:1-4*).
> (2) A declaration of one's Christian convictions and beliefs (*Romans 1:16; Matthew 10:32-33*).

Sin separated man from God, but Jesus through Calvary became man's mediator or bridge to God. Through the cross, man can be reconciled (made right) with God, and baptism tells the message of God's awesome love and sacrifice for the world:

> For God so loved the world that He gave His only begotten son that whosoever believeth on Him should not perish but have everlasting life. (John 3:16)

WHAT SCRIPTURE SAYS ABOUT BAPTISM

The Bible offers a number of clear teachings on baptism:

- Only those who are saved may be baptized (Acts 2:38);
- Immediately following a person's conversion he or she should be baptized (Acts 8:35-39);
- Failure to be baptized after salvation is an act of disobedience;
- Un-baptized believers cannot live with a "clear conscience" before God (1 Peter 3:21);
- Age is not a factor in relation to baptism, but salvation is;
- A believer need only be baptized once (Acts 16:31-33);
- Baptism is not proof of salvation (Acts 8:13, 23);
- Baptism is not essential to salvation (Romans 10:13; Ephesians 2:8-9);
- Believers must be baptized in the name of the triune God (Matthew 28:19).

Warren Wiersbe expands on the relationship of baptism to salvation:

> If baptism is essential for salvation, then nobody in the Old Testament was ever saved, for there was no baptism under the Law. Christ came to save, yet He did not baptize (John 4:2). If baptism is necessary for eternal life, why did Paul rejoice because he had not baptized more people? (1 Corinthians 1:13–17).[124]

SINCERITY OF HEART IN BAPTISM

Christians have recognized the significance of baptism since the very earliest days of the church.

BAPTISM
UNIT 6

The Didache: The Teaching of the Twelve Apostles, written in approximately 100 A.D., is the first instruction book for those to enter the church, and it explains what the believer is expected to believe and how he or she is to live. In the seventh chapter, it instructs a candidate for baptism to fast for two or three days prior to being baptized. While this is not mandated in Scripture, it shows the early Christians' determination to make sure that everyone who was baptized knew well what they were doing. This certainly suggests that believers today should ponder deeply the implication and meaning of baptism—whether in a time of fasting or just solitude before the Lord—prior to its observance. The person being baptized should enter the pool with grave sincerity, understanding what it means.

> **WORD WISDOM: REPENTANCE**
>
> The change of mind, belief, and direction toward God, motivated by "godly sorrow." Repentance means making a spiritual "about face" (*Acts 20:21; 2 Corinthians 7:10*), and it creates great joy in heaven (*Luke 15:7*).

REVIEW

(1) How does baptism speak to the unsaved? _____

(2) What are the two meanings of "confession"? _____
(3) Who should be baptized? _____ Who shouldn't? _____
(4) Why should a believer be baptized? _____
(5) Not being baptized after salvation is an act of _____.
(6) How often should a person be baptized? _____
(7) A person should be baptized in the name of the _____, _____, and _____.
(8) Because they were acutely aware of the significance of baptism, what did early Christians recommend as a way of preparing for baptism? _____

REFLECT—*Consider What This Means*

(1) What are the connections between confession, justification, adoption, and repentance? _____

(2) What does your own baptism mean to you? _____

(3) How does it make you feel to know that you belong to Jesus? _____

(4) If someone were to say to you, "I know I'm saved, so getting baptized isn't important," how would you respond? _____

GROWING IN KNOWLEDGE, LIVING BY FAITH
UNIT 6

RESPOND—*What Will You Do with What You Know?*

(1) If you have accepted Jesus as your Lord and Savior but have never been baptized, now is the time to do it, and it's not hard to arrange. Simply let your minister know that you want to be baptized in obedience to Christ. He will arrange a suitable time and handle all the details. Talk to your minister about it this week.

(2) Are there any adjustments you need to make in your thinking about baptism—the necessity of it, the way it should be done, the meaning of it, etc.? If so, note here what you need to change and find someone this week to whom you can explain your new way of thinking. _____
_____

(3) What are some ways in which you need to die to self (see below—"Neglect Not") _____
_____

(4) Do you know someone who needs to be baptized but who doesn't seem to be aware of it? If so, make it a point to talk with him or her this week and explain how important baptism is for a believer.

NEGLECT NOT: DAILY DYING TO SELF

"I die daily."
—1 Corinthians 15:31

If a spiritual giant such as Paul had to crawl upon the altar of death to self each day, how much more do you and I? Baptism in part symbolizes an initial dying to self in the life of a believer, but to grow spiritually, we must continue to die to self daily. The flesh will constantly seek to retake the throne in the believer's life, so every single day the first order of business is to crucify the flesh and its ungodly desires (Romans 6:6-13; John 12:24). A Christian must repeatedly present his or her total self to the Lordship of Christ to become a Romans 12:1-2 Christian. Spurgeon says it this way:

> Walk worthy of your high calling and dignity. Remember, O Christian, that thou art a son of the King of kings. Therefore, keep thyself unspotted from the world. Soil not the fingers which are soon to sweep celestial strings; let not these eyes become the windows of lust which are soon to see the King in his beauty—let not those feet be defiled in miry places, which are soon to walk the golden streets—let not those hearts be filled with pride and bitterness which are ere long to be filled with heaven, and to overflow with ecstatic joy.[125]

UNIT 7

THE LORD'S SUPPER

Years ago, I donated blood to a teenager who desperately needed blood of my type. The young man's name was Paul, and he was gracious about my "gift" to him. Once recovered, Paul said to me, "Frank, thank you for the blood." He knew my blood was a significant part of the treatment that had kept him alive.

As we look at Calvary through this study of the Lord's Supper, let's remember His shed blood that was poured out to enable us to have life abundant and eternal. Whenever we come to the table, our attitude should be: "Jesus, thank you for the blood."

> *In order that we might remember Him, Jesus didn't ask for a monument to be erected or a holiday to be established. He asked that a meal be enjoyed.*[126]
>
> —Jon Courson

THE TWO ELEMENTS

The elements of the Lord's Supper presented in Luke 22:18-19—"bread," representing Jesus' broken body and "the fruit of the vine," representing Jesus' spilled blood—point to the physical incarnation, sacrificial death, triumphant resurrection, and second coming of Jesus Christ. While neither element in any way transmits grace or cleanses the recipient of sin, both are meaningful components of the memorial Jesus left with his disciples in the Upper Room.

Referencing the bread, Jesus said, "Take, eat: this is my body." The bread is symbolic of Jesus' broken body for man's redemption, and one indisputable fact prevents us from taking His declaration literally. Jesus was alive when these words were spoken—still in the body—and nothing could be clearer to the Corinthians (1 Corinthians 11:23-26) than that Jesus' body and the bread were two completely different things.

Referencing the juice, Jesus said, "This cup is the new testament in my blood." Similarly, the juice is not the actual blood of Jesus nor does it become the literal blood when partaken. The juice simply symbolizes the redemptive work of Christ on Calvary. For those who take the bread and juice into their hands and upon their lips with faith and love, it stirs a vivid memory of the awesome love of God and the hefty price Christ paid for man's reconciliation.

> **WORD WISDOM: MESSIAH**
>
> "Anointed One" sent from God; Jesus the Christ. Christ means Messiah (*John 1:41; 4:35*). Jesus means Savior (*Matthew 1:21*).

The Bible does not cite any particular frequency for the observance of this Supper but simply states, "For as often as ye eat this bread, and drink this cup, ye do show the Lord's death till he come"

(Luke 22:26). The believer is worthy to partake of this Supper based not on personal merit but only on his or her relationship with Jesus Christ. Yet Jesus welcomes all of His children to His table (it's not the table of any specific church or denomination).

REVIEW

(1) What should be the attitude of anyone who partakes of the Lord's Supper? _____

(2) What do the two elements of this ordinance represent? _____

(3) Who may participate in the Lord's Supper? _____

(4) How often does the Bible recommend partaking of the Lord's Supper? _____

(5) "Messiah" means "_____."

PICTURES IN THE LORD'S SUPPER
(1 Corinthians 11:17-34)

"This do in remembrance of me." An array of important truths are depicted in the act of the Lord's Supper. Understanding each one will help you appreciate this memorial to Christ whenever you partake.

THE LORD'S SUPPER PICTURES CHRIST

The Lord's Supper is, above all, about the sacrificial death of Jesus on Calvary. Reflecting on the profound significance of Jesus' sacrifice should be foremost in the mind of those who partake. Jesus alerts believers to remember that it was He, the sinless Son of God, who paid the ultimate price for man's salvation. Apart from Him, salvation is simply not possible. When He calls us to remember this, Jesus is saying, "As often as you come to my table do not forget what I did at Calvary out of love for you."

THE PICTURE OF CALVARY

The Lord's Supper not only reveals the historic fact of Jesus' death but the manner of His death. He laid down His life at Calvary and bore its excruciating pain and death because of His love for the world. The Lord's Supper speaks of:

- The crown of thorns upon His brow;
- The nails that pierced His hands and feet;
- The sword thrust into His side;
- The spit hurled upon Him;
- All the accusations railed against Him.

THE LORD'S SUPPER

UNIT 7

All of these He endured to secure our salvation. We can envision the agony these physical acts of violence caused Him, but what about the "unknown suffering" Jesus bore in the inner chamber of the heart? He says to us, "Remember it! Don't ever forget!" The "bread and the fruit of the vine" declare, "Remember Calvary and all Jesus bore there for the forgiveness of man's sin."

> **WORD WISDOM: RESURRECTION**
>
> The rising from death to life—*not* the resuscitation—of Jesus (*Acts 4:33*) and at the end of the age, the raising of all the saints.

THE CELEBRATION PICTURED

The Lord's Supper is a feast, not a funeral! It's a party celebrating all Christ did for mankind at Calvary. Everything it says speaks of joy and hope. Matthew's account of the Lord's Supper states that this celebration included singing (Matthew 26:30). Let the redeemed of the Lord *sing* around His table songs of praise and adoration like:

> I heard an old, old story how a Savior came from glory
> How He gave His life on Calvary, to save a wretch like me.
> I heard about His groaning, and His precious blood atoning
> Then I repented of my sin and won the victory.[127]

In coming to the table, celebrate Jesus and what He has done that no one else could do for you.

THE LORD'S SUPPER PICTURES *COMMUNION*

Five times in 1 Corinthians 11, Paul refers to the "coming together" of believers—in verses 17, 18, 20, 33, and 34. The Lord's Supper is a time when God's people are truly united in focus and fellowship as they sit at *one* table, partake of *one* meal, and drink of *one* cup. The Lord's Supper pictures Christ's desire for the church to be *one* in devotion, doctrine, and duty, showing love *one* to another.

THE LORD'S SUPPER PICTURES *COMMISSION*

> **WORD WISDOM: GLORIFICATION**
>
> The state of perfection and total conformity to the image of Christ which occurs at the final resurrection (*Philippians 3:21; 1 John 3:2*). I await heaven not primarily for relief from trials nor reunion with saints but for release from this body of flesh ("corruption") that often disappoints God due to sin.

No clearer gospel message could be presented than Jesus' use of the bread and cup in speaking of man's salvation. It is a visible sermon of the message and meaning of the cross. It is a testimony to those who do not love Jesus of God's awesome love for them. The Lord's Supper teaches and reminds believers to proclaim its message to the world.

GROWING IN KNOWLEDGE, LIVING BY FAITH

UNIT 7

THE LORD'S SUPPER PICTURES *CONSUMMATION*

Jesus will come back to take those who love Him to His home in Heaven ("till I come"). This is a promise Jesus will keep (1 John 3:2-3). When coming to His table, believers are exhorted to "Look up for your redemption draweth nigh" (Luke 21:28).

THE PICTURE OF *CONFESSION*

As the believer prepares to partake of this meal, self-examination is crucial. The Lord's Supper is to be observed with clean hands, pure heart, and proper motive (1 Corinthians 11:27-29). A time of personal reflection before coming to the table often reveals acts of sin that must be confessed to Christ and cleansed before taking the elements (1 John 1:9). Jesus welcomes to the table all His children who meet this condition.

> Unworthy manner (11:27): *ritualistically, indifferently, with an unrepentant heart, a spirit of bitterness, or any other ungodly attitude.*[128]
>
> —John MacArthur

REMEMBER TO KEEP IT SPECIAL

In observing the Lord's Supper, remember these seven things with gratitude to Jesus for all He did to make possible "salvation so rich and free." Guard your approach against becoming mundane, ritualistic, and mere formality.

REVIEW

(1) What are the seven pictures presented in the Lord's Supper? _____

(2) Which picture should be foremost in the mind of a believer? _____

(3) Does the Lord's Supper possess saving power? _____ Why or why not? _____

(4) "Resurrection" and "resuscitation" mean the same thing.   ❏ True ❏ False ____

(5) When will believers experience glorification? _____

NEGLECT NOT: SELF-EXAMINATION

"Search me, O God."
—Psalm 139:23-24

In the same way King David examined himself, the Christian should pray regularly to detect sin, spiritual laxity, or heresy. Left unchecked, these problems will undermine a believer's walk with Christ. Spiritual "check-ups" are imperative to assure spiritual health. Leonard Ravenhill offers a wonderful prayer for self-examination:

> There is sin in the camp, there is treason today.
> Is it in me? Is it in me, O Lord?
> There's cause in our ranks for defeat and delay
> Is it in me, is it in me, O Lord?
> Something of selfishness, garments or gold,
> Something of hindrance in young and in old.
> Something as to why God's blessing He doth withhold.
> Is it in me, is it in me, is it in me, O Lord?[129]

The Christian should try to live so as to declare with Charles A. Tindley:

> Nothing between my soul and the Savior,
> So that His blessed face may be seen;
> Nothing preventing the least of His favor,
> Keep the way clear! Let nothing between.[130]

In the event of moral or spiritual failure, God stands ready to forgive, cleanse, and restore—just as He's done with David, the prodigal son, and myriad others (1 John 1:7-9).

GROWING IN KNOWLEDGE, LIVING BY FAITH
UNIT 7

REFLECT—*Consider What This Means*

(1) On a dirt road deep in the country a car struck and killed a boy riding his bicycle.
   His older brother reported, "Later, when my father picked up the mangled, twisted bike, I heard him sob out loud for the first time in my life. He carried it to the barn and placed it in a spot we seldom used. Father's terrible sorrow eased with the passing of time, but for many years whenever he saw that bike, tears began streaming down his face.
   "Since then I have often prayed, 'Lord, keep the memory of Your death as fresh as that to me! Every time I partake of Your memorial supper, let my heart be stirred as though You died only yesterday. Never let the communion services become a mere formality, but always a tender and touching experience.'"
   Consider whether or not your experience of the Lord's Supper is as fresh every time as the father of the boy killed on the bicycle. Describe how you experience Christ's table: _____
   _____
   If it's not all you think it should be, what would you like your experience to be? _____
   _____
   Make the prayer of the older brother your own.

(2) How do you experience the truth that the Lord's Supper is a "feast, not a funeral"? _____
   _____
   _____
   _____

(3) With John MacArthur's definition in mind: Are there ways in which you partake of the Lord's Supper in an "unworthy manner"? _____
   _____

(4) In the Lord's Supper, Jesus talked about His broken body and His shed blood. What might be some reasons He used two elements in His memorial instead of just one? (Note: The intent is simply to consider how the two elements make a stronger picture than one.) _____
   _____
   _____

RESPOND—*What Will You Do with What You Know?*

(1) Are there any unconfessed sins—perhaps even habitual ones—you need to confess before the next time you take the Lord's Supper? _____ During your prayer time this week, ask God to reveal to you anything from which you need to be cleansed before your next experience of the Lord's Supper.

(2) Have you ever donated blood? You might consider doing that (if your health allows) and use it as a time to think about the life-giving significance of blood and Jesus' willingness to give His blood for your sake.

(3) Find out when your church is planning the next celebration of the Lord's Supper. Mark the date on your calendar, and make absolutely certain you don't miss it.

UNIT 8

STEWARDSHIP

"One of the greatest missing teachings in the American church today is the reminder to men and women that nothing we have belongs to us."[131]

This profound observation from Gordon MacDonald stands as a glaring reminder that every person—no matter how high or low his or her socio-economic level—is a steward, not an owner, of possessions here on earth. In fact, even the idea of what constitutes a "possession" needs scrutiny in a study of stewardship.

A steward is someone entrusted to manage possessions that do not belong to him. And God has given people a variety of things to manage, not just the "stuff" we buy. According to Scripture everyone is a steward of his or her body, health, money, ability, gifts, and time and as such, is entrusted to make the wisest and most biblical use possible of these things (Psalm 24:1). It's a high calling.

Solomon instructs:

> Be not wise in thine own eyes: fear the LORD, and depart from evil. It shall be health to thy navel, and marrow to thy bones. Honour the LORD with thy substance, and with the firstfruits of all thine increase: So shall thy barns be filled with plenty, and thy presses shall burst out with new wine. (Proverbs 3:7-10)

> *Moreover it is required in stewards, that a man be found faithful.*
> —1 Corinthians 4:2

THE MACEDONIAN GIVERS

To study the requirements of stewardship, we'll take an in-depth look at one of Scripture's great examples of stewardship. In the New Testament, the believers to whom Paul wrote 2 Corinthians serve as a pattern of New Testament stewardship. We'll look at the characteristics of these outstanding stewards as revealed in 2 Corinthians 8:1-15.

THEY GAVE THEMSELVES

"But first they gave their own selves to the Lord" (verse 5).

These early saints made it a top priority to completely offer body, mind, and soul to God (Romans 12: 1-2). Total submission like theirs is the foundation of biblical stewardship from which the grace of giving springs.

I once heard a story that presents a delightful image of this total giving of self. During a revival in

GROWING IN KNOWLEDGE, LIVING BY FAITH

UNIT 8

Africa, the deacon taking up the offering presented the plate to a brand-new Christian. The young man smiled and told the deacon to hold the collection plate down lower.

"Lower," he said, "lower, lower"—until the offering plate was on the ground.
Then he stood up and stepped in. This man understood. He got the picture and gave himself.[132]

All believers would do well to follow this example. Through personal dedication to God, there will come a disciplined use of a believer's treasure, time, talent, and all he or she manages for Kingdom purposes.

THEY GAVE EAGERLY

"They begged us again and again for the privilege of sharing in the gift for the believers in Jerusalem" (verse 4, NLT).

The Macedonian saints literally begged for the privilege to give to the believers in Jerusalem. They viewed giving as an honor, not an obligation. As a young student pastor, I encountered this attitude from a widow in our church. At times, she begged me to accept monetary gifts from her. She longed to help her pastor financially and would not take "No" for an answer.

This attitude of eagerly wanting to give to the cause of Christ through the local church, a missionary, evangelist, ministerial student, or the poor is one all believers should exhibit, taking advantage of every opportunity to help God's work financially. You may not always be able to fully meet a financial or material need in a church or ministry, but you can steadfastly maintain an attitude of eagerness to do what is possible.

A young man received an eye-catching car as a gift, and a poor boy asked him, "Mister, where did you get that shiny red car?"
The youth responded, "My brother gave it to me."
Expecting the boy would respond, "I sure wish I had a brother like that," he was shocked instead to hear the reply, "Boy, I wish I could be a brother like that."
This little boy expressed the right attitude in giving.

> *If a person gets his attitude toward money straight, it will help straighten out almost every other area in his life.*[133]
> —Billy Graham

REVIEW

(1) Who is a steward? _____
(2) Name six things of which we are stewards, according to Scripture. _____
_____
(3) What does the story of the African Christian who stepped in the offering plate signify? _____
_____
(4) Christians should be _____ to give to God's work.

STEWARDSHIP
UNIT 8

THEY GAVE SACRIFICIALLY

"They are being tested by many troubles, and they are very poor. But they are also filled with abundant joy, which has overflowed in rich generosity" (verse 2, NLT).

Though experiencing great troubles and deep poverty, the Macedonian saints sacrificed greatly to meet the needs in Jerusalem. This reflects the reality that financial giving will always be a sacrifice because it involves some denial of personal, family, or business assets. Giving should always cost the giver something. Following a plague in Israel, God directed King David to build an altar on a threshing floor belonging to a man named Araunah and to make sacrifices there. Araunah offered to give the property and oxen for the sacrifice to David, but David refused:

> Nay; but I will surely buy it of thee at a price: neither will I offer burnt offerings unto the LORD my God of that which doth cost me nothing. So David bought the threshing floor and the oxen for fifty shekels of silver. And David built there an altar unto the LORD, and offered burnt offerings and peace offerings. (2 Samuel 24:24-25)

King David refused to give God that which cost him nothing. A gift's size and worthiness is measured by what it cost to give. Spurgeon emphasizes this point:

> Our gifts are not to be measured by the amount we contribute, but by the surplus kept in our own hands. The two mites of the widow were, in Christ's eyes, worth more than all the other money cast into the treasury, for "she of her want did cast in all she had, even all her living."[134]

> *When it comes to giving until it hurts, most people have a very low threshold of pain.*
>
> —Anonymous

While the Macedonians, David, and other faithful givers in the Bible model what our giving should look like, Christ's sacrifice is the ultimate example of sacrificial giving. Christ's unmatched generosity is our primary impetus and inspiration for giving. Paul described Jesus' offering for us: "For ye know the grace of our Lord Jesus Christ, that, though he was rich, yet for your sakes he became poor, that ye through his poverty might be rich" (2 Corinthians 8:9). Jesus was the most generous person who ever lived.

> *He [Jesus] was rich in possessions, power, homage, fellowship, happiness. He became poor in station, circumstances, in His relations with men. We are urged to give a little money, clothing, and food. He gave Himself.*[135]
>
> —Gordon MacDonald and Art Farstad

GROWING IN KNOWLEDGE, LIVING BY FAITH
UNIT 8

John MacArthur explains the immensity of our generous Christ:

> He laid aside the independent exercise of all His divine prerogatives, left His place with God, took on human form, and died on a cross like a common criminal, that you...might become rich. Believers become spiritually rich through the sacrifice and impoverishment of Christ. They become rich in salvation, forgiveness, joy, peace, glory, honor, and majesty. They become joint heirs with Christ.[136]

Isaac Watts captures Christ's sacrifice—and our only reasonable response—in his classic hymn "When I Survey the Wondrous Cross":

> When I survey the wondrous cross
> On which the Prince of glory died,
> My richest gain I count but loss,
> And pour contempt on all my pride.
>
> See from His head, His hands, His feet,
> Sorrow and love flow mingled down!
> Did e'er such love and sorrow meet,
> Or thorns compose so rich a crown?
>
> Were the whole realm of nature mine,
> That were a present far too small;
> Love so amazing, so divine,
> Demands my soul, my life, my all.[137]

THEY GAVE EXPECTANTLY

"Fellowship of the ministering of the saints" (verse 4).

The Macedonian saints believed God would use their gift to help suffering believers in Jerusalem and that He would also supply the Macedonian's needs as well (Philippians 4:19). Faithful giving not only advances the gospel but benefits the giver:

> Give, and it shall be given unto you; good measure, pressed down, and shaken together, and running over, shall men give into your bosom. For with the same measure that ye mete withal it shall be measured to you again. (Luke 6:38)

> *A man there was and tho some did count him mad; the more he cast away {gave} the more he had.*[138]
> —John Bunyan

Solomon declares, "The liberal soul shall be made fat: and he that watereth shall be watered also himself" (Proverbs 11:25). By this measure, the Macedonian saints were "fat."

STEWARDSHIP
UNIT 8

No one can out-give God. Captain Levy, a Christian from Philadelphia, was asked how he could give so much to the Lord's work and still possess great wealth. The Captain replied, "Oh, as I shovel out, He shovels in; and the Lord has a bigger shovel than I have."[139] Spurgeon offers similar testimony:

> In all of my years of service to my Lord, I have discovered a truth that has never failed and has never been compromised. That truth is that it is beyond the realm of possibilities that one has the ability to out give God. Even if I give the whole of my worth to Him, He will find a way to give back to me much more than I gave.[140]

REVIEW

(1) Why did King David insist on paying Araunah for his threshing floor and oxen? _____
_____
(2) How does God measure the size of our gifts? _____
_____
(3) Who was the most generous person who ever lived? _____
(4) Faithful giving not only advances the gospel but benefits the _____.
(5) What will God do for the giver? _____

THEY GAVE JOYOUSLY

WORD WISDOM: HALLELUJAH, ALLELUIA

The expression of joy, praise, or thanks to God. The literal meaning of the Hebrew *hallelujah* is "praise the Lord" (*Psalm 146*). The New Testament Greek equivalent is *alleluia* (*Revelation 19:1*). Augustine said "The Christian should be an alleluia from head to foot." As he lifts up one foot, a believer should shout "hallelujah" and as he brings it down, shout "praise the Lord."[141]

"The abundance of their joy" (verse 2).

The Macedonian saints did not give grudgingly or out of legalistic obligation. They gave joyously. Similarly, the privilege of financially supporting the cause of Christ locally and globally should bring joy to the believer. Paul encourages this attitude:

> Every man according as he purposeth in his heart, so let him give; not grudgingly, or of necessity: for God loveth a cheerful giver. (2 Corinthians 9:7)

THEY GAVE WILLINGLY

"They were willing... of themselves" (verse 3).

When asked how much milk his cow gives, a farmer replied, "If you mean 'voluntary contribution,' then she doesn't give anything, but we take from her eleven quarts a day."

GROWING IN KNOWLEDGE, LIVING BY FAITH
UNIT 8

I saw an amusing cartoon once that shows a man named Charles being baptized and the pastor saying to him, "Everything that goes under the water belongs to God." As the pastor lowers Charles under the water, Charles' hand extends out of the water clutching a wallet. He was not willing to give of his treasure to the Lord.

The Macedonian Christians were not "cow-like" or "Charles-like" givers. These saints did not give because they were pressured to. They were willing to give. Saints ought to submit all they have to God and give willingly, not out of compulsion or induced guilt.

THEY GAVE LOVINGLY

"I am not commanding you but testing the genuineness of your love by the enthusiasm of others." (verse 8, ISV).

> *God does not send you a bill. The church does not send you a bill. Giving to God and to the support of the work of the Kingdom isn't done in fulfillment of some "eleventh commandment." Your giving should be motivated by your love to God. How much you give of what you have should be a reflection of how much you love God.*[142]
>
> —Donald Whitney

The Macedonian Christians evidenced their love for God by their giving. A biblical test of a Christian's sincerity in loving God is giving. Generosity will overflow from the saint who truly loves God. Spurgeon explained this succinctly: "Giving is true loving."

Price Kellam, a saintly deacon in my student pastorate, refused to claim his financial gifts to the Lord's work as a tax deduction despite my effort to have him do so. To him, claiming tax deductibility would have contaminated his motive for giving which was based solely on his love for God.

> *Real charity doesn't care if it's tax deductible or not.*[143]
>
> —Anonymous

In giving, stay focused upon the true Recipient, Jesus Christ. You are giving to the King of Kings. Churches and ministries are merely conduits authorized by Him to receive and disburse His money.

> *Money never stays with me. It would burn me if it did. I throw it out of my hands as soon as possible, lest it should find its way into my heart.*[144]
>
> —John Wesley

THEY GAVE SYSTEMATICALLY

"Now concerning the collection for the saints, as I have given order to the churches of Galatia, even so do ye. Upon the first day of the week let every one of you lay by him in store, as God hath prospered him, that there be no gatherings when I come." (1 Corinthians 16:1-2)

STEWARDSHIP
UNIT 8

Although in 2 Corinthians 8 Paul did not specifically address the manner in which the Macedonians were to give, it stands to reason they were to give as he instructed the Galatians (and others) regarding the same offering for the Jerusalem Christians who were suffering due to famine. Note Paul's three-fold instruction regarding their giving:

(1) It was to be received systematically on the first day of the week, Sunday.
(2) It was to be corporate giving—everyone was to participate in the offering.
(3) It was to be proportionate giving—the amount was to be based on how God hath prospered him, in keeping with an individual's income and resources.

This passage summarizes for all believers how they should give:

- Giving should be intentional and systematic;
- All are to give;
- Giving should be based upon the measure in which God has financially blessed.

George Muller emphasized the power and necessity of regular giving:

Are you giving systematically to the Lord's work, or are you leaving it to feeling, to impression made upon you through particular circumstances, or to striking appeals? If we do not give from principle systematically, we shall find that our one brief life is gone before we are aware of it, and that, in return, we have done little for that adorable One who bought us with His precious blood, and to whom belongs all we have and are.[145]

There are two ways in which a Christian may view his money—"How much of my money shall I use for God?" or "How much of God's money shall I use for myself?"[146]

—W. Graham Scroggie

REVIEW

(1) How did the Macedonians evidence their love for God? _____

(2) What is the benefit of giving systematically? _____

(3) What three points summarize how Christians should give? _____

(4) Who is the true recipient of the gifts a Christian gives? _____

(5) What does George Muller caution that we will lose if we don't give systematically? _____

GROWING IN KNOWLEDGE, LIVING BY FAITH
UNIT 8

THE STARTING BLOCK FOR GIVING IS THE TITHE

The Bible teaches tithing. A tithe is one tenth of your income.
That one-tenth of your income belongs to the Lord. In addition
to your tithe, you should give as the Lord has prospered you.[147]
—Billy Graham

In the Old Testament, there were several mandatory tithes the people were to give to the Lord:

- The Levite's tithe—10 percent, Malachi 3:10;
- The Festival tithe—10 percent, Deuteronomy 12:10-11;
- The tithe for the Poor—3 percent, Deuteronomy 14:28-29.

In addition, the people were to give free will offerings for special projects. Taken together, these combined acts of giving reveal that the people of God in the Old Testament were giving between 27 and 40 percent of their income to God's work.[148] With that perspective, our contemporary concept of the tithe as 10 percent (30 percent less than Old Testament givers!) should be considered a *starting* point for the believer's giving. Galatians 3:24 reminds us of the place for Old Testament teaching in our lives: "The law is a tutor to lead us toward Christ."

Much has been said of giving a tenth of one's income to the Lord.
I think that is a Christian duty which none should, for a moment,
question. If it was a duty under the Jewish Law, much more is it
so now under the Christian dispensation.[149]
—Spurgeon

The tithe as part of the Old Testament Law serves as a teacher prompting the believer to start with 10 percent of income and seek to give more. The tithe is the floor level of giving, not the ceiling (Haggai 2:8). Donald Whitney offers a probing thought to help the believer examine what he or she should be giving:

When we put a check or cash in the offering plate, we should give it with the belief that all we have belongs to God and with a commitment that we will use all of it as He wants.[150]

Quite simply, Christians need to learn to live with less so that more money may be given to evangelism and mission endeavors.

I do not believe one can settle how much we ought to give. I am
afraid the only safe rule is to give more than we can spare.[151]
—C. S. Lewis

STEWARDSHIP
UNIT 8

REVIEW

(1) What does Billy Graham suggest the believer should give besides the tithe? _____

(2) What are the three tithes commanded in the Old Testament? _____

(3) How does the Old Testament "tutor" us in giving? _____

(4) According to Donald Whitney, whose money is it, anyway? _____

(5) What is C. S. Lewis's rule for giving? _____

THE VALUE OF GIVING

The benefits of giving are clearly presented in Scripture.

GIVING PLEASES THE SAVIOR

In giving her two mites, the widow of Mark 12:42-43 pleased the Lord. The woman of Bethany who anointed Jesus' feet with ointment pleased Him (Luke 7:37-47). The little boy in John 6:9-13, by giving his loaves and fishes, pleased the Lord. These individuals gave what they could give, and Christ is always pleased when His children give what they can "according to how God hath prospered him" (1 Corinthians 16:2).

GIVING PROVIDES FOR THE SAINT

The giver has a clear scriptural promise that giving results in bountiful provision. Jesus declares:

> Give, and it shall be given unto you; good measure, pressed down, and shaken together, and running over, shall men give into your bosom. For with the same measure that ye mete withal it shall be measured to you again. (Luke 6:38)

Matthew Henry expands on this point:

> *Men* shall *return it into your bosom (lap)*; for God often makes use of men as instruments, not only of his *avenging*, but of his *rewarding* justice. If we in a right manner give to others when they need, God will incline the hearts of others to give to us when we need, and to give liberally, *good measure pressed down and shaken together*. They that sow plentifully shall *reap plentifully*.[152]

> **WORD WISDOM: AMEN**
>
> An expression of hearty approval (*1 Chronicles 16:36*).

In Malachi 3:8-10, God promises to open the windows of heaven upon the giver, pouring out blessings to the extent "that there shall not be room enough to receive it." Solomon also explains the miracle of receiving as a result of giving:

GROWING IN KNOWLEDGE, LIVING BY FAITH

UNIT 8

> There is that scattereth, and yet increaseth; and *there is* that withholdeth more than is meet, but it *tendeth* to poverty. The liberal soul shall be made fat: and he that watereth shall be watered also himself. (Proverbs 11:24-25)

The more you give, the more you will get. But note that in these texts God does not indicate the type of provision that will be returned. The writer of Hebrews assures the giver:

> God is fair; he will not forget the work you did and the love you showed for him by helping his people. And he will remember that you are still helping them. (Hebrews 6:10, NCV)

GIVING PRODUCES SOULS

Godly giving funds churches, missionaries, and evangelists, enabling the proclamation of the gospel locally and globally. A song by Ray Boltz reflects the value of such giving:

> Then another man stood before you, he said
> "Remember the time,
> A missionary came to your church, His pictures made you cry.
> You didn't have much money but you gave it anyway.
> Jesus took that gift you gave
> And that's why I'm in Heaven today."
> Thank you for giving to the Lord,
> I am a life that was changed.
> Thank you for giving to the Lord,
> I am so glad you gave.[153]

WORD WISDOM: TEMPTATION

(1) An enticement or lure to do evil. Satan and his demons tempt all mankind to disobey God, but God tempts no man to evil (*James 1:12-15*). Deliverance from temptation is possible (*1 Corinthians 10:31; Matthew 6:13*). (2) A time of testing from God to prove devotion and commitment while strengthening the saint's faith (*Genesis 22:1-19; Job 1-2; 1 Peter 1:3-9*).

There's a story about a $100 bill and a $1 bill on the way to the furnace (the place all old money is destined). The $1 bill asks the $100 bill how its life has been. "Really great," it replies, "I made a lot of trips to San Francisco, to the finest department stores and restaurants. Been good." The $100 bill, in turn, asks the $1 bill, "How about your life?" The $1 bill replies, "My life was pretty much giving to church, giving to church, giving to church."

The story shares a simple—but unfortunate—reality. Far too many saints give generously at restaurants, department stores, and vacation resorts but only miserly to God's work. To all of us, though, the wondrous possibility presents itself that by giving generously and regularly to God, many more souls will hear the Good News of Christ throughout the world, resulting in lives being eternally changed.

In Luke 19:11-27, Jesus shares the parable of the talents. Upon his departure for a lengthy trip, a master entrusts one talent to one of his servants, two talents to another, and five talents to a third. Upon the master's return, each servant must give an account of how he used the money. This story presents a picture of Jesus entrusting His children (servants) with money to manage Kingdom business (Deuteronomy 8:18; James 1:17). Jesus has departed for a time for heaven but upon His return, He will require an accounting by every servant for the worthy or unworthy use of His money (Luke 19:13).

STEWARDSHIP
UNIT 8

REVIEW

(1) What are the three primary values of giving? _____
_____

(2) Christ is always pleased when His children give what they can "according to how God _____
_____ him."

(3) What does Scripture promise to those who give? _____

(4) What eternal benefits can result from giving to Kingdom work? _____
_____

(5) Who is represented by the master in the Luke 19:11-27 parable? _____ Where has He gone? _____ What will He do when He returns? _____
_____

REFLECT—*Consider What This Means*

(1) On a lecture circuit, a man demonstrated his awesome grip by squeezing all the juice out of an orange. Each time, he challenged his audience: "I will give $25 to anyone who can squeeze this orange and get more juice out of it." Although many tried, no one could extract more juice until one day a weak-looking man succeeded. Shocked, the lecturer asked him, "You don't look that strong. How in the world did you do that? What kind of work do you do?" The man responded, "I'm a Baptist preacher—I've had lots of practice squeezing things!"
Have you ever felt "squeezed" to give? Is that because you were receiving undue pressure from outside or because you were resisting from within?

(2) How are giving joyously, willingly, lovingly, and systematically related? _____
_____

(3) Does anything in your heart "contaminate" your motive for giving? _____
_____

(4) In what way is "hallelujah!" an appropriate response when you give to others? _____
_____

(5) What is the lifestyle of your $100 bills? _____ $1 bills? _____
_____

(6) How is not giving a temptation? _____ Do you struggle with that temptation? _____

RESPOND—*What Will You Do with What You Know?*

(1) Decide in your heart how much to give—and don't give reluctantly or in response to pressure. "For God loves a person who gives cheerfully." (2 Corinthians 9:7, NLT)

(2) Many churches provide members with offering envelopes, an excellent tool to assist in regular, consistent giving. If your church has them available, get some you can use routinely.

(3) Read the scriptures noted in this unit that reference the three tithes commanded in the Old Testament. Consider the intent of where these tithes were to be given and find godly places you

can give to meet similar needs.
(4) If you're not tithing, start with this small step: No matter how you receive your income—salary, tips, bonuses, business profits—resolve to give 10 percent of whatever comes to you this week. Regardless of how much or how little it amounts to, put that in the offering plate next Sunday.
(5) Do #4 again the next week.

NEGLECT NOT: STEWARDSHIP

But this I say, He which soweth sparingly shall reap also sparingly; and he which soweth bountifully shall reap also bountifully. Every man according as he purposeth in his heart, so let him give; not grudgingly, or of necessity: for God loveth a cheerful giver.
—2 Corinthians 9:6-7

Water God's garden with monetary offerings, and God will water your garden financially or otherwise. Although you may say you cannot afford to give, God says you can't afford *not* to give. The story of three quarters teaches the lesson "little is much when God is in it":

Three quarters were talking among themselves about how they expected to be used. The first quarter said, "I'm going to be used to buy some candy for Jimmy to make him happy." The second explained, "I'm going to buy Timmy some marbles to make him happy." And the third added, "I'm going to be put into the offering plate by Tommy to help purchase a truck for a missionary." The other quarters laughed saying, "What can one little quarter do to buy a truck that costs $20,000?"

The candy purchased with the first quarter disappeared in a few bites. The marbles from the second quarter for Timmy were lost after a game or two. But in time, enough money was raised to buy the missionary truck, and the quarter that helped buy it was still at work years later delivering materials to missionary outposts.

So where will you put your quarter? The writer of Hebrews exhorts:

Let us, then, always offer praise to God as our sacrifice through Jesus, which is the offering presented by lips that confess him as Lord. Do not forget to do good and to help one another, because these are the sacrifices that please God. (Hebrews 13:15-16, GNT)

Stewardship represents not only the proper use of a believer's treasure but also his or her time and talent (Romans 12:1-2). Don't neglect giving of your tithes and offerings to the Lord.

UNIT 9

SATAN

Satan is for real.

The Bible is unequivocal in teaching that Satan truly exists. W. A. Criswell dramatically emphasizes this truth:

> He is called by his name 174 times in the Word of God. He's called Satan. He's called the Devil. He's called that old serpent. He's called the dragon. He's called Beelzebub....he is presented as a person, a personality, as somebody, like God is somebody, like Michael is somebody, like Gabriel is somebody. This enemy of ours is somebody. Eve met him in the Garden of Eden. Job had to do with him. He fell into the hands of Satan....Christ himself addressed him as Satan: "Satan, get behind me!" A personal enemy.[154]

> *The devil is delighted to be denied! He doesn't want to be given credit for a job well done! He resists detection. He doesn't desire your consideration....But remember you cannot defeat an enemy as long as you deny him. Face the foe! Find out who he is! Force him to acknowledge the truth! Fight the fight of faith and watch him FLEE!*[155]
>
> – Jack R. Taylor

When a person comes to salvation and renounces the old life of sin and religious formality, Satan cunningly plots the believer's downfall. His intent is to drag the new believer back down into the mire of sin from which he or she was rescued.

> *"Though Satan instills his poison, and fans the flames of our corrupt desires within us, we are yet not carried by any external force to the commission of sin, but our own flesh entices us, and we willingly yield to its allurements."*[156]
>
> —John Calvin

Scripture cautions us—by admonition and by example—not to underestimate our enemy's power to bring a Christian down. If the adversary can destroy a Samson, a David, and a Demas, any one of us are vulnerable (Judges 16:18-21; 2 Samuel 11:3-5; 2 Timothy 4:10). Paul cautions, "Let him that thinketh he standeth take heed lest he fall" (1 Corinthians 10:12). And Peter warns, "Be sober, be vigilant; because your adversary the devil, as a roaring lion, walketh about, seeking whom he may devour" (1 Peter 5:8).

GROWING IN KNOWLEDGE, LIVING BY FAITH
UNIT 9

Satan is characterized in vivid terms in Scripture:

- The "slanderer" tries to accuse Christians falsely before God and use the unsaved to do the same. The word "devil" means to "slander."
- A "serpent" seeks to deceive believers as he did Eve in the garden (2 Corinthians 11:3).
- A "lion" seeks to "devour" (totally consume) the believer's spiritual vitality, testimony, and witness (1 Peter 5:8).
- The "wellspring of lies" seeks to deceive man by counterfeiting salvation and "sugar coating" the consequence of a life apart from God (John 8:44).
- The "destroyer" (Revelation 12:11) "seeks to kill, steal and destroy" the best of a person's life (John 10:10).

Satan is relentless in his attempts to shipwreck a believer's life and witness. Don't be surprised to find yourself regularly under attack. Peter exhorts the believer to "resist Satan steadfastly in the faith" (1 Peter 5:9). Christians must stay alert, watchful for Satan's ploys to trip him up by standing firm in the Word of God.

> *The devil is against us, the world is around us, and the flesh is within us, collaborating to defeat us in our Christian walk.*[157]
> —Jerry Rankin

The schemes of the devil include:

- Lying (John 8:44);
- Tempting (Matthew 4:1);
- Robbing (Matthew 13:19);
- Harassing (2 Corinthians 12:7);
- Hindering (1 Thessalonians 2:18);
- Sifting (Luke 22:31);
- Imitating (2 Corinthians 11:14-15);
- Accusing (Revelation 12:9-10);
- Smiting with disease (Luke 13:16);
- Possessing (John 13:37);
- Killing and devouring (John 8:44).

> **WORD WISDOM: DEMONS**
>
> Evil spirits (fallen angels) who are the servants of Satan. There is one Devil and many demons (*Ephesians 6:12*). Demons may *oppress* the saint but cannot *possess* the saint.

As if the accounts of Satan and his work are not enough to make clear the reality of his influence in the world, Scripture also assigns an array of descriptive names and titles to our opponent:

- Satan—the opposer (Matthew 4:10, Revelation 12:9; 20:2);
- Devil—the accuser (Matthew 4:1, Ephesians 4:27);
- Lucifer—the shining one (Isaiah 14:12; 2 Corinthians 11:14);
- Anointed cherub—the lofty ranking among angels which he held prior to his fall (Ezekiel 28:14);
- Evil one—the personification of evil (Matthew 13: 19, 38; John 17:15);
- Ruler of this world—the one who presides over the evil world system of men and de-

mons; Jesus called Satan this three times (John 12:31; 14:30; 16:11);
- God of this age—the blinder of minds regarding the gospel (2 Corinthians 4:4);
- Prince of the power of the air—the pervasive one (John 12:31; Ephesians 2:2);
- Serpent—the deceiving and devious one (Genesis 3:1, 2 Corinthians 11:3);
- Dragon—the fiercest one possessing power to destroy (Revelation 12:3, 7-9);
- Accuser—the accuser of the saint before God (Revelation 12:10);
- Deceiver—the counterfeiter of truth and right (Revelation 12:9; 20:3);
- Murderer—the one who brought death to Adam and the whole human race (John 8:44; Genesis 3:1-7);
- Liar—the wellspring of untruth (John 8:44);
- Sinner—the first sinner (1 John 3:8);
- Beelzebub—the ruler of a demonic host (Matt. 10:25; 12:24, 27; Luke 11:15);
- Belial—the "worthless" or "wicked" one (2 Corinthians 6:15);
- Roaring lion—the hungry evil one whose appetite devours the believer (1 Peter 5:8).

REVIEW

(1) Satan is a mythological character.   ❏ True   ❏ False
(2) Is there biblical evidence that Satan is a real being? _____ If so, summarize it here: _____
_____
(3) What is Satan's primary intent toward believers? _____

VICTORY OVER SATAN

How can a Christian overcome the tactics of Satan? Ephesians 6:11-18 teaches that wearing the right protection is the answer.

As a baseball catcher, I wore "armor" that consisted of a chest protector, shin guards, mask, and a glove. This protection kept me from serious injury so I could stay in the game. Just as athletes need protection in the games they play, Ephesians 6 says believers need spiritual armor to protect them in the game of life.

> *The only time to stop temptation is at the first point of recognition. If one begins to argue and engage in a hand-to-hand combat, temptation almost always wins the day.*[158]
> —Thomas a' Kempis

THE BELT OF TRUTH

The belt reinforces the believer's need to live his belief. To do that, Christians daily study the Bible and try to live what it teaches. This Belt of Truth holds other pieces of the armor together, giving the soldier freedom of movement. The Belt of Truth holds the believer's life together when things shatter and crumble around him or her, and Satan tries to restrict a Christian's freedom to press onward.

THE BREASTPLATE OF RIGHTEOUSNESS

The breastplate reflects the believer's need to start each day clean and holy. The believer's first act of business each morning is to get right before God. No Christian should carry soiled laundry (sin) into a new day but start fresh and pure.

THE GOSPEL SHOES

Shoes demonstrate the believer's assurance of salvation and his or her willingness to plunge in to whatever duty is required. It is important that Christian soldiers walk in full confidence of salvation so in the time of doubt or temptation they will not stumble and fall. Confidence of salvation enables a life of peace in every circumstance of life, whether good or bad. Gospel shoes also remind saints of the need to share the Good News of the Gospel with the unsaved.

THE SHIELD OF FAITH

The shield speaks of the believer's need to continuously believe God. Genesis 3 records Satan's lie to Eve:

> "You won't die," the serpent hissed, "God knows that your eyes will be opened when you eat it. You will become just like God, knowing everything, both good and evil." The woman was convinced. The fruit looked so fresh and delicious, and it would make her so wise! So she ate some of the fruit. (Genesis 3:4-6, NLT)

The root cause of Eve's trouble is that she believed Satan over God. Her shield came down, and sin entered the world. Don't be like Eve—always believe God.

Every Roman soldier was responsible for providing some measure of protection for comrades in battle, so he carried the shield on his left arm so it protected two-thirds of his own body and one-third of the body of the solider on his left. Likewise, Christians are to protect each other by exhibiting faith. This not only serves the one who demonstrates faith but encourages other Christian soldiers who come alongside them.

> *I often laugh at Satan, and there is nothing that makes him so angry as when I attack him to his face, and tell him that through God I am more than a match for him.*[159]
> —Martin Luther

THE HELMET OF SALVATION

The helmet shows the need to look at the finish line in heaven. The Helmet of Salvation reminds believers there is a finish line ahead where Jesus waits for the saved. This part of the armor assures the

> Two types of swords are mentioned in the New Testament. One was huge with a blade 40 inches or more (*romphaia*) and the other was much smaller with a blade of anywhere from 6 inches to 18 inches (*macharia*). The *romphaia*, gripped with two hands by a Roman soldier, was used in battle when precision work was not required; the *macharia* being lightweight was easily wielded in combat to fend off assault and to make a precise thrust. The type of sword to which Paul refers in Ephesians 6:17 is the *macharia*. He does not mention the huge sword that took two hands and was used without much precision.
>
> John MacArthur surmises, " The principle that Paul is clearly presenting in Ephesians 6:17 is that when using the sword of the Spirit, we need to be specific. When temptation comes we cannot simply wave the Bible in the air vand say, 'God's Word will protect me!' We need to know which part of God's Word fits the situation. We need to know how to use the sword of the Spirit on defense and offense."[160]
>
> —John MacArther,
> *Why Believe the Bible*

believer of salvation and that one day he or she will be in the eternal presence of the King of Kings. This helmet also protects the believer's mind from being dominated by carnal and sensual thoughts.

THE SWORD OF THE SPIRIT

The sword represents the power of Holy Scripture in the believer's life. In His wilderness temptations, Jesus used the Sword of the Spirit (the Word of God) to drive back Satan, declaring, "It is written…" (Matthew 4:1-11). "It is written" is a dagger to Satan's heart. During temptation, believers should quote scripture that forces Satan to flee—hence, the importance of scripture memorization (Psalm 119:11).

THE KNEES OF PRAYER

> **WORD WISDOM: MILLENNIUM**
>
> A period of 1000 years in which Jesus with His saints will reign on earth and Satan will be bound (*Revelation 20:7; Zechariah 14:4-5, 9*).

"Praying always with all prayer and supplication in the Spirit, and watching thereunto with all perseverance" (Ephesians 6:18) is Paul's final direction in this passage about Christian armor. It is a reminder that success in spiritual battle is simply not possible apart from the divinely infused strength gained through prayer. The preacher George Allen Smith once stood on a precipice in the Alps, drinking in the view of Switzerland, when a blast of wind threatened to blow him over the edge. His guide cried out, "Mr. Smith! On your knees, sir! The only way you're safe up here is on your knees!"[161] Similarly, when battling Satan, the only way you're safe here is on your knees.

REVIEW

(1) What are the seven pieces of armor a Christian is to put on daily in order to be victorious over the schemes of the devil? _____
_____

GROWING IN KNOWLEDGE, LIVING BY FAITH
UNIT 9

(2) What does each piece of armor do for a believer? _____
_____
_____
_____
_____

PRAYING ON THE ARMOR OF GOD

To put on the Armor of God, a believer needs to pray it on. It is an encouraging and fruitful exercise to do this literally each day. You might want to try using a prayer similar to the one I use:

> Heavenly Father, thank You for the armor provided for my victory today. By faith, I put on the Belt of Truth that I might live what I believe and advocate. Keep me from being a castaway by helping to maintain my integrity. By faith, I put on the Breastplate of Righteousness that I may start this day clean and holy, prepared to live a life pleasing to You. By faith, I put on the Gospel Shoes that I may be surefooted in battle against Satan, assured of my salvation and my eternal destiny, and ever ready to serve. By faith, I put on the Shield of Faith trusting You to extinguish the fiery darts of opposition that Satan hurls upon me. I will not fear what may happen today for Thou art a shield of protection unto me. By faith, I place the Helmet of Salvation upon my head to protect my mind from carnal thoughts and to focus on the completion of my salvation in heaven. Lord, today I look for Your coming and my departure to heaven. By faith, I pick up the Sword of the Spirit, Thy Holy Word, to drive Satan back and to overcome

THE GOSPEL ARMOR
(FRANK SHIVERS)

Christian warrior put on the Gospel Armor from head to toe, that victory may be won against Satan, the able foe.

Belief and practice must agree, lest the believer be a poor witness of one set free.
This Belt of Truth prompts self-discipline in the spiritual fight and enables the believer's *Light* to ever glow bright.

Purity in heart assure at day's start, making it the goal not to depart.
This breastplate protection from despair due to sin will bring,
Prompting joyfulness, and fruitfulness unto the King.

Gospel shoes give security when peace about salvation is attacked,
Granting calm assurance it's a certain fact.

Faith is the victory that overcomes the world,
Raise this shield of defense when Satan's fiery arrows of doubt, difficulty and discouragement are hurled.

The helmet of salvation place upon the head,
It assures of union with Christ and heaven that waits ahead.

Wield the Sword of Scripture at Satan when with him in fight,
And he will have no recourse but to take quick flight.

No armor for the back reveals the believer isn't to turn and run,
But faithfully fight the battle 'til Satan is defeated and the victory is won.

Each day for warfare the believer is to prepare
By putting on this armor in fervent prayer.

temptation. By faith, I pray each piece of this protective armor upon my life that I may be a victorious Christian soldier. Grant it, O Lord, I pray, in Jesus' name. Amen.

Martyn Lloyd-Jones reinforces the necessity that Christians wear all the armor:

> If you are to be a soldier in this army, if you are to fight victoriously in this crusade, you have to put on the entire equipment given to you. That is a rule in any army. . . . And that is infinitely more true in this spiritual realm and warfare with which we are concerned . . . because your understanding is inadequate. It is God alone who knows your enemy, and He knows exactly the provision that is essential to you if you are to continue standing. Every single part and portion of this armour is absolutely essential; and the first thing you have to learn is that you are not in a position to pick and choose.[162]

"While Satan is a decided fact, a destructive force—praise the Lord—he is a defeated foe!"[163]

—Stephen Olford

PRACTICAL DISCIPLINES FOR CLAIMING VICTORY OVER SATAN

As in any war, soldiers need a battle plan. I've outlined below the Christian's plan for victory in the fight with Satan.

ANTICHRIST—SATAN'S "BLACK OPS" STRATEGY

The term "antichrist" is a subject of much discussion with regard to end times. Many people wonder "who the antichrist will be." But the biblical term "antichrist" has much more depth than that simple guessing game suggests. Scripture uses "antichrist" in three ways:

(1) The final great opponent of Christ—a rival "Christ" who will be revealed at the start of the Great Tribulation (*Matthew 24:24; Mark 13:22*). The title itself is found only in John's epistles (*e.g., 1 John 2:18*). M. R. Vincent explains that:

> While the false Christ is merely a pretender to the Messianic office, the Antichrist "assails Christ by proposing to do or to preserve what he did, while denying Him." Antichrist, then, is one who opposes Christ in the guise of Christ.[164]

Antichrist is a person (*Revelation 13; 16; 19*) who will surface as a world leader possessing such charisma, charm, and conniving ability that he convinces people to follow him, to replace Christ with himself.

(2) Antichrists. John warns that many antichrists are now on the scene and more shall arrive (*1 John 2:18*). Anti-Christian teachers who denounce Jesus as the Savior of the world (*1 John 2:22*) and endeavor to seduce believers (*1 John 2:26*) into believing a lie are deceivers and forerunners to te Anti-christ

(3) The spirit of Antichrist (*1 John 4:3*). Jon Courson explains:

> The spirit of antichrist has pervaded human history. For example, as the atrocities of Hitler and Stalin continue to come to light, the only explanation for their murderous insanity is the spirit of antichrist attempting to destroy God's people, and, in Stalin's own words, to become "the new Christ."[165]

GROWING IN KNOWLEDGE, LIVING BY FAITH

UNIT 9

- *Feed on the scripture regularly.* The intake of megadoses of God's Word builds spiritual muscle to resist the wiles of the devil.
- *Memorize scripture.* David testifies, "I have hid thy word in my heart that I might not sin against thee" (Psalm 119:11). Scripture was the weapon Jesus used to defeat Satan in the wilderness and will likewise be yours. Start memorizing verses that specifically address areas of greatest vulnerability.
- *Engage in persistent and passionate prayer.* Prayer links you to the Divine power needed to thwart the attack of the enemy.
- *Enlist a fellow believer to hold you accountable.*
- *Rely upon the super-duper-natural strength of Jesus Christ* to drive Satan and the demons back (Philippians 4:13).
- *Maintain intimate communion and fellowship with Christ.*
- *Avoid people, places, and pleasures that present a temptation.* Don't give Satan a beachhead into your heart (Ephesians 4:27).
- *Attend church faithfully.*

REVIEW

(1) How do you put on the armor of God? _____

(2) According to Martyn Lloyd-Jones, who is the only one who really knows the enemy? _____

(3) What reason does the poem "The Gospel Armor" give for there being no back in the set of armor? _____

(4) What eight disciplines help assure victory over Satan? _____

(5) Explain three meanings of "antichrist"? _____

WORD WISDOM: ARMAGEDDON

Literally means "Mount of Megiddo," a small mountain overlooking the Mediterranean Sea. Joel prophesies that in this valley a war like none other will occur between the forces of righteousness (God) and Satan in the end time (*Joel 3:12; Revelation 16:16*).

NEGLECT NOT: THE SECOND COMING

"Looking for that blessed hope, and the glorious appearing of the great God and our Savior Jesus Christ, who gave Himself for us."
—Titus 2:13

Have you been waiting, working, and watching expectantly for Christ's coming? Prior to going to bed each night, the last action of Dr. Horatius Bonar, Scottish preacher and hymn-writer, was to draw back the drapes and look into the starry sky, asking, "Perhaps tonight, Lord?" Similarly, Bonar's first action each morning was to lift the blind, look out on the morning dawn and ask, "Perhaps today, Lord?"[166]

As Bonar, in an effort not to *neglect* the second coming of Christ, I discipline myself each morning to spread my arms toward the heavens and say, "Lord, today help me to look for your appearing and live accordingly."

H. A. Ironside was also clear on the importance of looking for Christ's coming again:

> To profess to hold the doctrine of the premillennial coming of Christ is one thing. To be really held by it is quite another. He whose life is unrighteous, whose spirit is worldly, and whose outlook on life is carnal and selfish has never yet learned to love His appearing.[167]

Early saints kept this doctrine foremost in their own minds as well as that of other believers by sharing the greeting, "Maranatha, Maranatha"—"The Lord comes, the Lord comes," referencing Revelation 22:20. We should do likewise today.

REFLECT—*Consider What This Means*

(1) Read about how Peter (Matthew 26:58, 69, 70), Demas (2 Timothy 4:10), and Thomas (John 20:27) were vulnerable to Satan. What are your areas of vulnerability? _____

(2) How might it encourage another believer to see you standing firm in your faith? _____

(3) Read aloud the poem "The Gospel Armor" and pause as needed to consider both where you need strengthening and where you've seen victories. Pray for strengthening and thank God for your victories.

(4) How does remembering the Lord's Second Coming help defeat Satan in daily living? _____

RESPOND—*What Will You Do with What You Know?*

(1) Do you fully accept the Bible's teaching about the reality of Satan? If not, ask God to help you grow in your awareness of your personal enemy.
(2) If you aren't doing so already, put on the armor of God (use the prayer in this unit) every day for the next week. See if you notice any difference in the success of your walk with Christ.
(3) Review the "disciplines for victory" as if it is a checklist on how you're doing. If you find areas needing improvement, make it a point to do better in that respect this week.

UNIT 10

WITNESSING

The great contemporary evangelist Bailey Smith shares a revealing story about the life-and-death importance of sharing Christ (my paraphrase):

> Years ago two families resided in Kentucky. One had the only radio for miles around. This family heard that a tornado was heading straight for their neighbor's house, so the father sent his son Merle to give warning. Merle darted out the door to do just that, but a bird landed on a limb, and he stopped to throw a stone at it. He missed. He then started running to fulfill his mission again when the bird flew back to another limb close to him. This time his rock was right on target, and the bird fell to the ground. As he picked up the bloody bird, he heard a rushing sound coming from the direction of the Renfro family's home in the valley—the family he was to warn. He looked toward it just in time to see their four bodies thrust to death. He rushed back to tell his father what had happened. In the midst of the story, his father noticed blood on the boy's hands and asked him what that was. Merle told him it was the blood of the bird he killed. His father replied, "No, son, that's not the blood of the bird you killed. It is the blood of the Renfro family you failed to warn."[168]

> *The other things we have to do may be called important by those around us, but there is nothing on earth more important to do than to win a person to Jesus Christ.*[169]
>
> —Bailey Smith

Far too many believers are guilty of throwing stones at birds while people all around them die and go to hell—and their hands are dripping with the blood of those they could have brought to salvation! The goal of this study is to challenge you not to be distracted by "birds" (lesser things) but instead, to diligently seek to share Christ with all who need the warning of the eternal peril they face without Him. Scripture is clear that one day believers will be held accountable for those to whom they had the chance to witness but didn't (Ezekiel 33:7-9). What you do or don't do now is unalterable for eternity.

THE FIVE CALLS TO WITNESS

In Acts 1:8, Jesus exhorts all believers to be His "witnesses." A witness is one who tells the truth about something that he or she has experienced firsthand. Jesus wants those of us who are saved to simply tell our own stories of salvation and relate it to the message and meaning of His death, burial, and resurrection (Matthew 10:32-33; 1 Peter 3:15). The Bible tells us five ways in which Christians are called to fulfill Jesus' command to be His witnesses.

> **WORD WISDOM: DEPRAVITY**
>
> Corruption, immorality, wickedness of man at the core of his being. It necessitates Divine intervention and remedy (*Romans 7:18*).

GROWING IN KNOWLEDGE, LIVING BY FAITH
UNIT 10

THE CALL FROM *ABOVE*

Christ on His throne in heaven calls the saved to be His witness:

- "Ye shall be witnesses unto me both in Jerusalem [home area] and in all Judea [state] and in Samaria [across America] and unto the uttermost parts of the earth [everywhere else]" (Acts 1:8);
- "I have chosen you, that you should go and bring forth fruit" (John 15:16);
- "Follow me and I will make you fishers of men" (Matthew 4:19).

The Lord's command is crystal clear: *Go and tell.*

THE CALL FROM *AROUND*

Broken, bleeding, bound, and blind souls are crying out for help. Their body language and lifestyles are but a plea for you to tell them of Him who alone can make the eternal difference in their lives.

THE CALL FROM *WITHIN*

In the heart of the saved is the voice of the Holy Spirit pleading, "Go and tell of Calvary's love and Jesus' desire to save from sin." Indeed, with Paul the saint cries, "The love of Christ constraineth me" to go and tell.

God plants within the soul of all He saves the desire to reproduce. In fact, the person who has no desire to tell is not "born of Him" (Matthew 10:32-33). W. A. Criswell explains, "The first impulse of a born-again Christian is to win somebody to Jesus. If we lose this drive, we are untrue to the Holy Spirit within us and we deny the great will of God for us."[170]

I understand that a person may work hard at soulwinning but never win a soul (though highly unlikely), but I will never understand how a person who claims to know Christ could never witness. It just doesn't mesh with what Scripture teaches. In the Bible, record after record is given about how those who Jesus saved immediately began to go and tell. Among these were Philip, Andrew, and the woman at Jacob's Well. The saved cannot but speak out loud for their Savior. He places within them a "divine heartburn" for the lost.

> *I would like to ask what right a man has to call himself a follower of Jesus Christ if he is not a soul-winner? There is absolutely no such thing as following Christ unless you make the purpose of Christ's life the purpose of your life.*[171]
> —R. A. Torrey

THE CALL FROM *BELOW*

A call rings loud and clear from the torment and darkness of hell for the saved to be witnesses. Luke 16 tells the story of a man who died and went to hell. From his place of torment, he cries to

WITNESSING
UNIT 10

Abraham in heaven: "I pray thee therefore father, that thou wouldest send him to my father's house; for I have five brothers; that he may testify unto them, lest they also come to this place of torment." This man begged for someone on earth to warn his brothers lest they die in their sin and end up there with him.

> *If we only lead one soul to Jesus Christ we may set a stream in motion that will flow when we are dead and gone.*[172]
>
> —D. L. Moody

THE CALL FROM *THE FUTURE*

The certainty of death—yet its uncertainty as to when, where, or how—calls the believer to win others now lest they meet death unprepared. The brevity of life and the ever-decreasing opportunity for man to be saved urgently prompts the Christian to engage in soulwinning. The Holy Spirit empowers, emboldens, and enables you for witnessing (Acts 4:31-32). He will use you to communicate the gospel effectively to the unsaved.

REVIEW

(1) Explain the eternal significance of the story of the boy with bird blood on his hands. _____

(2) What is the meaning of the term "witness"? _____
(3) What is needed to remedy the depravity of mankind? _____
(4) For what does Ezekiel 33:7-9 say believers will be held accountable? _____

(5) In what four "regions" does Jesus tell believers they should be His witnesses? _____

(6) Where do the five calls to witness come from? _____

(7) Who empowers the believer to witness? _____

METHODS OF WITNESSING

> *Methods of evangelism alone can't convince someone to repent and turn to Christ. Only God can do that by applying His truth to the person's heart. Your task is to faithfully proclaim His truth and be sensitive to His Spirit's leading. Are you doing that?*[173]
>
> —John MacArthur

There are many ways to share the Gospel effectively with others. In my book *Soulwinning 101*, I share 275 helps for winning the lost to Christ. Several "rise to the top," though, and prove to be especially useful for a wide range of sharers as well as hearers. I include here four of the simplest and most tried-and-true methods.

Bear in mind that, regardless of the method utilized, it is essential to avoid religious jargon unfamiliar to unbelievers. William Faulkner, referring to Ernest Hemingway, offers a winsome guideline in this regard: "He has never been known to use a word that might send a reader to the dictionary."[174] Christians must try to do the same when speaking with non-believers.

PERSONAL TESTIMONY

> *Unregenerate man will neither understand nor believe the Gospel without the work of the Holy Spirit. Man is in need of both objective revelation of the Gospel (disclosed by Christ and the Scripture) and subjective illumination (enlightenment about Christ and need of salvation) by the Holy Spirit. Seek the Holy Spirit's guidance and power in soulwinning. Pray for His illumination of the truth of Christ, sin, judgment and things to come to those to whom the message of Christ is shared.*

One of the greatest methods of witnessing is to use your own salvation testimony (My Story). A personal witness should include five specific points and should be easily shared in three to five minutes. Fine-tune the story of your conversion so it is simple enough that "even a cave man can understand it." The following outline of the Apostle Paul's testimony to King Agrippa serves as an excellent model for personal testimony (Acts 26:3-29):

(1) My life before meeting Christ (Acts 26:3-11);
(2) How I came to realize my need of Christ (Acts 26:12-14);
(3) What I did to become a Christian (Acts 26:15-18);
(4) My life since I became a Christian (Acts 26:19-23);
(5) Appeal—Would you be willing to do as I did and receive Jesus Christ into your life as Lord and Savior (Acts 26:27-29)?

> *Oh, to realize that souls, precious, never-dying souls, are perishing all around us, going out into the blackness of darkness and despair, eternally lost, and yet to feel no anguish, shed no tears, know no travail! How little we know of the compassion of Jesus!*[175]
>
> —Oswald J. Sanders

COLORS OF SALVATION CARD

With these laminated cards, a color symbolizes each of nine truths about salvation on one side and the explanation of each on the other. I've found that the graphic appeal makes it effective with children, youth, and adults and as a result have made them available through the Frank Shivers Evangelistic Association (FSEA) at www.frankshivers.com. Here's what the colors mean:

WITNESSING
UNIT 10

- *Black* stands for man's sin against God that resulted in separation and condemnation. Sin is disobeying God and failure to keep His commandments. Sin separates a person from God now and in eternity. As Romans 6:23 states, "The wages (consequences) of sin is death." And no one is exempt: "All have sinned and fallen short of the glory of God" (Romans 3:23). Everyone is in the same boat spiritually and in need of a Savior.

- *Red* symbolizes the blood of Jesus Christ shed at Calvary in response to man's desperate need and God's amazing love. The Apostle John says, "The blood of Jesus Christ cleanses from all sin" (1 John 1:7), and in John 3:16 declares, "For God so loved the world (you) that He gave His only begotten son that whosoever (you) believes on Him should not perish but have everlasting life."

- *White* signifies the soul's cleansing upon repentance and faith in Jesus Christ. The condition of salvation (forgiveness) is "repentance toward God and faith in the Lord Jesus Christ" (Acts 20:21). To repent is to change one's mind about both the sin which he has committed and the place he gives God in life.

- *Blue* represents the open confession of Christ in believer's baptism. Baptism does not save a person. A person is baptized because he or she is saved (Matthew 10:32-33).

- *Green* reminds us of the disciplines essential for spiritual growth. Once a person receives Christ as Savior and Lord, he or she is as a "newborn babe" requiring help to grow up in Christ Jesus. Scripture urges the believer to "grow in the grace and knowledge of our Lord and Savior Jesus Christ" (2 Peter 3:18). Spiritual disciplines for growth include prayer, intake of the Word, solitude, worship (private and corporate), witnessing, and giving.

- *Purple* declares the Lordship of Christ in the believer's life. Jesus is to be "Lord of all." Acts 10:36 states, "The word which God sent unto the children of Israel, preaching peace by Jesus Christ (He is Lord of all)." Jesus' Lordship in a person's life means He is in total control, both inside and out.

- *Yellow* represents the saint's faithful service to Christ. Christians are to be "faithful unto death." John admonishes, "Fear none of those things which thou shalt suffer: behold, the devil shall cast some of you into prison, that ye may be tried; and ye shall have tribulation ten days: be thou faithful unto death, and I will give thee a crown of life" (Revelation 2:10).

- *Gold* stands for the believer's eternal home in heaven. Heaven awaits the child of God at the end of life's journey. In speaking of heaven, Jesus said, "In my Father's house are many mansions: if it were not so, I would have told you. I go to prepare a place for you. And if I go and prepare a place for you, I will come again, and receive you unto myself; that where I am, there ye may be also" (John 14:1-3).

- *Gray* symbolizes the Valley of Decision in which the unsaved reside. The prophet Joel cries, "Multitudes, multitudes in the valley of decision in the day of the Lord" (Joel 3:14). The Lord calls on man to make a decision concerning personal sin and his relationship to Him.

GROWING IN KNOWLEDGE, LIVING BY FAITH

UNIT 10

THE ROMAN ROAD

The plan of salvation I use most often because of its near-universal effectiveness is the Roman Road method. It's also the first soulwinning method I ever used.

The Road centers around six brief passages in the book of Romans and explains the steps to salvation:

1. Romans 1:3-4 (also reference John 3:16)—Tell them the Who of Salvation
2. Romans 3:23—Tell them the What of Salvation
3. Romans 6:23—Tell them the Why of Salvation
4. Romans 5:8; 10:9-13—Tell them the Way of Salvation
5. Romans 10:13; (also 2 Corinthians 6:2)—Tell them the When of Salvation

To simplify using the Roman Road, I recommend marking these verses in your New Testament and noting the order in which to use them.

TRACT LADDER

A friend introduced me to the Gospel Tract Ladder nearly forty years ago. It's a simple but effective use of tracts that progresses from easy to more difficult stages in sharing the gospel. Imagine a ladder with six rungs that take you through the steps described below.

Rung 1: Leave a Tract. This first step in witnessing works even for the "faint of heart." It requires no courage since it can be done secretly. You simply distribute gospel tracts in places like restrooms, bus stations, restaurant menus, or magazines.

Rung 2: Mail a Tract. This rung entails some boldness but not a lot. You insert a gospel tract in bill payments and correspondence.

> **WORD WISDOM: ETERNAL SECURITY**
>
> The true believer is eternally saved (*John 6:37*). John MacArthur points this out in his commentary on Jude 1:
> > That phrase can be translated…"kept by Jesus Christ." The Greek verb is *tereo*, which means "to watch, stand guard over, or keep." It stresses a watchful care to guard something as cherished as a priceless treasure. Do you know how secure I am? Just as secure as the power of the Lord Jesus Christ who keeps me. That is a fantastic concept! This keeping is permanent.[176]

Rung 3: Pin and Tract. Wear a large bold-colored badge or pin that prompts others to ask what it means. When asked, simply say, "Oh, it's to remind me to give you this tract that tells how much God loves you."

Rung 4: Hand a Tract. In this step, you hand a tract to someone and ask the person to read it at his or her leisure.

Rung 5: Lend a Tract. With this step, you give a tract or book to an unsaved person asking that he or she read and return it as soon as possible. This applies pressure on the unsaved person to read the material and provides an opportunity to discuss it when the material is returned.

WITNESSING
UNIT 10

Rung 6: Share a Tract. This rung requires the most boldness because you not only hand a tract to a person but explain it with the intention of bringing him or her to a decision for Christ.

For all steps, be careful to choose your tracts wisely. Make sure they are biblically sound and spiritually dynamic. FSEA offers tracts that meet these criteria.

> *When preaching and private talk are not available, you need to have a tract ready… a touching gospel tract may be the seed of eternal life.*[177]
>
> —C. H. Spurgeon

REVIEW

(1) What are the five points you should make when sharing your personal testimony? _____

(2) Name the "Colors of Salvation" and explain their meaning. _____

(3) What are the five W's in the Roman Road to salvation? _____

(4) What are the six rungs of the Tract Ladder? _____

ENEMIES OF SOULWINNING

Soulwinning is a challenge for many reasons, but there are seven readily identifiable enemies of soulwinning that we must combat:

(1) *Misunderstanding.* Satan wants saints to believe that winning souls is the task of the minister and church staff, not a responsibility assigned by Christ to all the redeemed (Acts 1:8).

(2) *Pessimism.* The mindset of many believers about witnessing is "it won't do any good." Yet our Lord said that "the fields are white (ripe) unto harvest"—people are hungering and thirsting for something missing from their lives, without which there is no real peace or purpose (John 4:35).

(3) *Busyness.* The pastor has sermons to prepare, administrative chores, and hospital visits, and the church member has his job, family engagements, and the social calendar. The noble desire to witness is buried beneath a load of daily duties, and so it goes undone. Christians should plan their day around soulwinning rather than soulwinning around the day. Keep it as a priority. C. H. Spurgeon made time each day to win a soul to Christ.

(4) *Unconcern.* Many Christians don't win souls simply because they lack passion and compassion for the eternally damned. Pray for a passion for souls as did George Whitefield, who said, "O God give me souls, or take my soul."[178]

(5) *Fear.* The Apostle Paul experienced fear (1 Corinthians 2:3). All believers do. It's neither unnatural nor unspiritual. The key is not to allow fear to paralyze and deter our soulwinning efforts. Paul didn't. We mustn't.

(6) *Carnality.* Spurgeon declared, "Fish will not be fishers. We cannot be fishers of men if we remain among men in the same element with them."[179] The "separated" Christian is the soulwinning Christian (2 Corinthians 6:17).

(7) *Imperceptibility of Hell.* A failure to grasp the destiny of the lost lessens concern and, thus, soulwinning. Hell is a reality, and it awaits the unsaved at the end of this life. Clear apprehension of hell as the end for unbelievers answers soberly the question, "Does it really matter if I try to lead others to Christ?"

> **WORD WISDOM: INHERITANCE**
>
> Believers are "joint heirs" with Jesus by divine relationship, inheriting every possession that belongs to Him (*Romans 8:17; Hebrews 1:2; 2 Peter 1:3-4; 2 Corinthians 1:20; Ephesians 1:11-12*)—that means *everything*.

> **WORD WISDOM: ELECTION**
>
> Election refers to people who choose to come to Christ. As Adrian Rogers explains:
> - "Who are the elect? The elect are the whosoever wills (*Revelation 22:17*)."[180]
> - "I do not see where it [the Bible] teaches God pre-selects some to salvation and consigns the rest of humanity to eternal damnation without ever making them a sincere offer of forgiveness."[181]

Whatever your doctrine of election is, if it intentionally or unintentionally slows you down in the task of confrontational evangelism, you've yet to discover what the Bible teaches about election.[182]

—Paige Patterson

C. H. SPURGEON'S SALVATION STORY

British pastor and theologian C. H. Spurgeon shares the passion which only a vivid personal testimony offers:

When the Lord first pardoned my sin, I was so joyous that I could scarce refrain from dancing. I thought on my road home from the house where I had been set at liberty, that I must tell the stones in the street the story of my deliverance. So full was my soul of joy, that I wanted to tell every snowflake that was falling from heaven of the wondrous love of Jesus, who had blotted out the sins of one of the chief of rebels. But it is not only at the commencement of the Christian life that believers have reason for song; as long as they live they discover cause to sing in the ways of the Lord, and their experience of his constant lovingkindness leads them to say, "I will bless the Lord at all times: his praise shall continually be in my mouth."[183]

WITNESSING
UNIT 10

REVIEW

(1) What are the seven enemies of soulwinning? _____
_____

(2) With whom are we "joint heirs" of God? _____

(3) In his personal testimony, Spurgeon points out that believers "have reason for song" more than just at the beginning of their walk with God. How long does this reason last? _____

(4) Who are the elect? _____
_____

NEGLECT NOT: SOULWINNING

> "But ye shall receive power, after that the Holy Ghost is come upon you; and ye shall be witnesses unto me both in Jerusalem, and in all Judea, and in Samaria and unto the uttermost part of the earth."
> —Acts 1:8

Jesus is saying, "Do not neglect witnessing." But sadly, many Christians do!

I was on my way to preach and noticed the words on a pontoon boat that read, "Go" (on the left pontoon) and "Fish" (on the right pontoon). I challenge you to "Go Fish"—fish for souls in the "pond" of your campus, neighborhood, dormitory, or job. Jesus said, "He that winneth souls is wise" (Proverbs 11:30)—not those who simply preach, sing, or teach. Speak out loud for Christ in solitude or in the multitude, in the daylight or twilight, in the bliss of life or the throes of death (Romans 1:16). Spurgeon described the breadth of Christian witness:

> It is well to preach as I do, with my lips; but you can all preach with your feet, and by your lives, and that is the most effective preaching. The preaching of holy lives is living preaching. The most effective ministry from a pulpit is that which is supported by godliness from the pew.[184]

A boy fell out of a boat and cried to his father, "Throw me a rope." The dad threw the only rope he had. The son cried, "Dad, the rope is too short. Throw me a longer rope." There was no longer rope to be thrown. The boy's last words to his dad were, "Dad, the rope's too short; throw me a longer rope." God is saying to Christians, "Throw out a longer rope to those perishing in the lake of sin." As you go among non-believers, resolve to throw out a longer rope, to increase your efforts, and to expend your energies in reaching the unsaved.

GROWING IN KNOWLEDGE, LIVING BY FAITH
UNIT 10

REFLECT—*Consider What This Means*

(1) W.E. Sangster says, "The simplest way to embarrass a normal congregation is to ask them two ordinary questions: 1. When did you last lead someone to Christ? 2. When did you last try?"[185] At the risk of embarrassing you, answer both questions. _____ _____ If you're unsatisfied, unsettled, or upset with the answers, let it spur you to greater effort in soulwinning.

(2) The saved cannot help but speak out loud for their Savior. He places within them a "divine heartburn" for the lost. Do you hear this call from within the citadel of your own heart to go and tell?

(3) Read Luke 16:19-31, the story mentioned in "The Call from Below" (p. 97). Do you hear pleas from hell begging you to witness to a son, a daughter, a spouse, or a friend? A passion for souls must overwhelm you, or you will never be serious about soulwinning.

(4) Muse over the nature of hell until your heart is inflamed to go and tell.

(5) Which of the enemies of soulwinning gives you the most trouble? _____

(6) Read Acts 8:26-40, and consider what Philip's encounter with the Ethiopian can teach you about witnessing. Make your observations here: _____ _____

RESPOND—*What Will You Do with What You Know?*

(1) Look at your hands. Is the blood of a friend, an acquaintance, a stranger, or a family member on them? If there's someone you know you should be sharing the Gospel with, don't let this week go by without doing it. If you need accountability, tell a Christian brother or sister who you need to share with and when. Ask your accountability partner to pray for you and for the person you want to reach.

(2) Outline the five points of your personal testimony, and share it with a non-believer.

(3) Get a copy of *Soulwinning 101* (available online at www.frankshivers.com), and read further about various approaches to personal evangelism. Decide which methods you would like to try in your own witnessing. Then try them.

(4) If you haven't done it yet, mark the Roman Road in the Bible you carry with you most often and practice using it.

(5) Purchase a package of gospel tracts (for example, "False Hopes of Heaven" at www.frankshivers.com), and try a few rungs of the Tract Ladder.

(6) Nearly 6,000 people die every hour without Christ, so every Christian should be urgent about telling others of their need to be born again. You may be someone's only roadblock on the road to hell. Brazen up, and tell of Jesus to them before it's too late.

(7) During the next month, read one of the following books on soulwinning:
- *The Soulwinner,* C. H. Spurgeon
- *Words to Winners of Souls,* Horatius Bonar
- *How to Give Away Your Faith,* Paul E. Little
- *The Master Plan of Evangelism,* Robert E. Coleman
- *Drawing the Net,* O. S. Hawkins

UNIT 11

CHURCH

"God's people are not dogs, else they might go about one by one; but they are sheep, and therefore they should be in flocks."[186] —C. H. Spurgeon

Gathering together is essential to the spiritual health of believers. Scripture exhorts Christians not to neglect corporate worship with other believers (Hebrews 10:25). The Greek word for church is *ekklesia*, which comes from the Greek verb *kaleo* ("to call") and the preposition *ek* ("out"): "the called out ones." *Ekklesia* also may be translated as "assembly" because it was a word used to describe a people who were "called out to a meeting."

> **WORD WISDOM: CHRISTIAN**
>
> This term is greatly misused when referring to one's culture, church, religious upbringing, or belief. It means "to belong to Christ and to have a personal relationship with Christ as Lord and Savior." Believers were first called Christians in Antioch (*Acts 11:26*).

The word "church" is found 115 times in the New Testament—and 92 of those times it means the local congregation. The church is not brick and mortar but people of common faith who have been saved and called out to worship and serve God (Colossians 1:13). Every believer needs the encouragement, instruction, correction, guidance, training, and support the church affords through the born-again ones of which this "Bride of Christ" consists. Billy Graham points out this unique function of the assembling together of Christians: "The Church has a very specific assignment, and only the church provides the nurture for spiritual growth."[187]

CHURCH MEMBERSHIP

What church should a believer join? There's not always a ready-made answer to that question because not all churches are biblical in belief and practice. Many churches look similar on the outside, but inside—the teaching, fellowship, doctrinal positions, governing practices—there can be radical differences. It's important to search out a church that unapologetically preaches and practices the whole teaching of the Bible, as well as one that is mission-minded and evangelistic.

Here are some benchmarks of the kind of church you want to look for:

(1) Truly biblical churches will proclaim:
- The deity of Jesus Christ;
- His virgin birth and virtuous life;
- Jesus' vicarious death, victorious resurrection, and verifiable ascension;
- His visible return to earth one day.

(2) A church should welcome "the good, the bad, and the ugly"—spiritually and physically.

(3) A church should view itself as a hospital for sinners and not a museum for saints.

GROWING IN KNOWLEDGE, LIVING BY FAITH

UNIT 11

WORD WISDOM: CHURCH

The church is primarily the local assembly of baptized believers in Jesus Christ (*Acts 5:42*). The Greek word for church is *ekklesia* which means "the called out ones" or "assembly."

To expand on this last point, a hospital is a place in which caring people take care of sick people, not condoning sickness but endeavoring to heal it. As a spiritual hospital, the New Testament church renders love, forgiveness, and care to the sin-sick, compassionately and without exception. While it embraces all people in love, it never sanctions or condones the acts of sin they commit. The Church seeks to "reprove them" so they may become spiritually whole.

The best churches are not satisfied with the "status quo" of ministry and membership but have an enthusiastic and challenging vision for the future (Proverbs 29:18). You'll want a church that has a good "feeding trough," where the pastor and Sunday school teachers serve nourishing, fortifying, and challenging spiritual meals. You'll not want to be in a church where, in the words of the poet John Milton, "the hungry sheep look up and are not fed."[188]

To help evaluate where a church stands in its ministry, outreach, and teaching, it is wise to review a copy of the church's constitution and covenant before making a decision about membership.

"THE CHURCH" ACCORDING TO THE *BAPTIST FAITH AND MESSAGE 2000*

"A New Testament church of the Lord Jesus Christ is an autonomous local congregation of baptized believers, associated by covenant in the faith and fellowship of the gospel; observing the two ordinances of Christ, governed by His laws, exercising the gifts, rights, and privileges invested in them by His Word, and seeking to extend the gospel to the ends of the earth. Each congregation operates under the Lordship of Christ through democratic processes. In such a congregation each member is responsible and accountable to Christ as Lord. Its scriptural officers are pastors and deacons. While both men and women are gifted for service in the church, the office of pastor is limited to men as qualified by Scripture. The New Testament speaks also of the church as the Body of Christ which includes all of the redeemed of all the ages, believers from every tribe, and tongue, and people, and nation."

REVIEW

(1) Gathering together is essential to the _____ _____ of the believer.

(2) What does the Greek word "ekklesia" mean? _____ _____

(3) Where were believers first called Christians? _____ _____

(4) What four things does a truly biblical church preach? _____ _____

(5) As a "spiritual hospital," how does the church treat sin-sick people? _____ _____ What is its view of their sin? _____

(6) Who is eligible to join a New Testament church? _____ _____

WHY GO TO CHURCH

We've already noted that attending church is essential to the spiritual growth of the believer, but there are a number of very specific reasons why this is true. Let's look at them.

GO TO GROW

Believers attend the Sunday school and worship services of the church in order to grow and abound in the things of God (Hebrews 10:25). No campus ministry, television evangelist, or Sunday broadcast can substitute for the Christian's involvement in the local church. C. H. Spurgeon points out that the spiritual foundation of attending church is obedience to God's command:

> Now, I know there are some who say, "Well, I hope I have given myself to the Lord, but I do not intend to give myself to any church, because—" Now, why not? "Because I can be a Christian without it." Now, are you quite clear upon that? You can be as good a Christian by disobedience to your Lord's commands as by being obedient? I do not believe it, Sir! Nor do you either.[189]

GO TO SHOW

Dedication to a local church is a witness to the world of a believer's allegiance to Jesus Christ (Matthew 16:18).

GO TO KNOW

In the church, believers are aligned with people who love Jesus and "spur" each other onward in the Christian journey both in word and example (Acts 2:42). The giant Redwoods, which have shallow root systems, withstand the force of mighty storms by intertwining their roots with each other. Young believers in particular have shallow spiritual roots and will surely falter under Satanic assault unless their roots are intertwined with mature believers in the church. Christian businessman Rich DeVos offers an imaginative picture of the fallacy of not fellowshipping with other believers:

> Some people think of their spiritual life as if they were one person in a telephone booth, talking to God on a private line. They don't want to be bothered by the demands of "organized religion" and don't think they need anyone else. "Oh yeah, I'm spiritual," they say, "I just don't like church." To those folks I say: "You cannot grow spiritually in isolation."[190]

GO TO BESTOW

Scripture emphasizes the believer's need to join the Body of Christ in worship. David declares in Psalm 5:7, "But as for me, I will come into thy house in the multitude of thy mercy: and in thy fear will I worship toward thy holy temple." Psalm 149:1 exhorts, "Praise ye the LORD. Sing unto the LORD a new song, and his praise in the congregation of saints."

GROWING IN KNOWLEDGE, LIVING BY FAITH

UNIT 11

Both private and corporate worship...are taught in Scripture, and the vitality and genuineness of corporate worship are to a large degree dependent upon the vitality of our individual private worship.[191]
—Jerry Bridges

To worship God is to ascribe to Him the supreme worth that He alone is worthy to receive.[192]
—Church Administration

> **PSALM 100:1-4**
>
> Make a joyful noise unto the LORD, all ye lands.
> Serve the LORD with gladness:
> come before his presence with singing.
> Know ye that the LORD he is God:
> it is he that hath made us, and not we ourselves;
> we are his people, and the sheep of his pasture.
> Enter into his gates with thanksgiving,
> and into his courts with praise:
> be thankful unto him, and bless his name.

A primary purpose in attending church is to engage in the corporate worship of God, bestowing on Him the sacrifice of praise and thanksgiving with lips of adoration. Worship is responding to God's graciousness, goodness, and being. It must not be confined to Sunday at church. Believers are to worship God with lip and life (externally and internally), both inside and outside the church by living a life oriented to His purpose and pleasure.

GO TO *SOW*

The church is a place of service (Ephesians 2:10; Matthew 28:18-20). A person is not saved to laze around but to get up and get going for God! In and through the varied evangelistic and missionary ministries of the church, believers can make a difference for eternity in the lives of others locally—and even globally—by giving financially, witnessing, praying, and serving in various capacities.

A soldier was separated from his unit and finally joined the ranks of another army regiment. He immediately asked an officer, "What can I do?"

"Fall in anywhere," the officer replied, "there's good fighting all along the line."

That's good advice for the new believer with regard to service in the church: "Fall in anywhere, for both inside and outside the walls of the church there is plenty of ministry to do." In his comments on 1 Samuel 13:20, Spurgeon put our need for assembling in the context of the spiritual war we are fighting:

> We are engaged in a great war with the Philistines of evil. Every weapon within our reach must be used. Preaching, teaching, praying, giving, all must be brought into action, and talents which have been thought too mean for service, must now be employed. Each moment of time, in season or

> **"THIS ONE THING I DO."**
>
> This reveals a key reason why the Apostle Paul was successful in Christian service (Philippians 3:13). Too many believers are tackling too many spiritual tasks. You can spread yourself so thin that nothing is really gained in anything. A turning point in the great evangelist D. L. Moody's life followed the Chicago fire in 1871 when he decided to follow Paul's example. Prior to the fire, Moody was involved in Sunday school promotion, Y.M.C.A. work, evangelistic crusades, and a host of other ministries; but after the fire, he decided to focus solely on the work of evangelism. "This one thing I do" enabled this evangelist to impact millions for Jesus Christ.[193]

out of season; each fragment of ability, educated or untutored; each opportunity, favorable or unfavorable, must be used, for our foes are many and our force but slender.[194]

According to L. A. Drummond, every believer possesses at least one spiritual gift to use in service to the Lord. He explains that there are nineteen categories of gifts cited in Scripture (in 1 Corinthians 12, Ephesians 4, and Romans 12). In the contemporary church, one person may be adept at teaching children's Sunday school while another may be able to teach more in depth as a pastor.[195]

In *The Canvas Cathedral,* Drummond explains the five ways Billy Graham encourages believers to discover their giftedness:

> (1) Realize they do have at least one spiritual gift. Some may well have more, but all have at least one.
> (2) Pray to discover spiritual giftedness.
> (3) Be willing to use spiritual gifts to bring honor to Christ and blessings of the Lord to the church.
> (4) Explore what the Bible says about the spiritual gifts, searching out examples of how they are employed.
> (5) Acquire a knowledge of their own self and abilities.
> Finding out may be a lengthy process, but it is the basis for any believer's service to the church. It is also crucial to recognize that all gifts are necessary and none are inherently better than others.[196]

Even if you lack a deep desire to work, you can fuel your own desire by simply starting somewhere. Volunteer! Your church will take it from there.

GO TO *GLOW*

A growing Christian is a glowing Christian. Glowing believers radiate the likeness of Christ in word and deed (Matthew 5:14-16). Others "take knowledge that they have been with Jesus" (Acts 4:13), testify regarding "Sir, we see Jesus" (John 12:21), and "I perceive that this day a holy man of God, who passeth by us continually" (2 Kings 4:9). The ministry of the church enables the Christian to be both "examples to all that believe" (1 Thessalonians 1:7) and penetrating lights to those in spiritual darkness (Luke 11:36; Proverbs 4:18; Isaiah 42:6).

> *Church attendance is as vital to a disciple as a transfusion of rich, healthy blood to a sick man.*[197]
>
> —D. L. Moody

GROWING IN KNOWLEDGE, LIVING BY FAITH

UNIT 11

REVIEW

(1) What are the six reasons for *going to church*? _____
_____

(2) How can a believer discover his or her spiritual gift(s)? _____
_____
_____

(3) According to Ephesians 2:10, the church is a place of _____.

(4) Jerry Bridges asserts that the quality of corporate worship depends in large measure on what? __
_____

THE AUTHORITY AND SPIRITUAL OFFICES OF THE CHURCH

Jesus Christ is "head of the church" (Colossians 1:18), but men are the stewards of Christ in His Church. While ultimate authority resides only with Christ, Scripture designates certain "offices" through which men manage the responsibilities to care for God's people.

> **WORD WISDOM: RAPTURE**
>
> "Caught up," the bodily transport of believers to heaven at Christ's second coming (*1 Thessalonians 4:14-17*).

The Office of Pastor—Ephesians 4:11 and 1 Peter 5:2-4

The primary role of the teaching pastor is to feed, equip (train), protect, and shepherd the flock of God. W. A. Criswell explains the background:

> In the New Testament sense, there are three words to describe the office of your preacher: episkopos, presbuteros, and poimen. Episkopos is translated "bishop" in our language; presbuteros is translated "elder;" and poimen is translated "pastor." And here in the New Testament, all three of those words refer to the same office, to the same man. He's a bishop; he's an elder; he's a pastor.[198]

The pastor serves as the "shepherd" of the church as ordained and sanctioned by God. John MacArthur said if he were to sum up his role as pastor and elder it would be this: "win, teach, train, and send."[199]

> *A church should be pastor-led, deacon-served, committee-operated and congregationally-approved.*[200]
> —Adrian Rogers

The Apostle Paul says of the pastor, "And we beseech you, brethren, to know them which labor among you, and are over you in the Lord, and admonish you; And to esteem them very highly in love for their work's sake" (1 Thessalonians 5:12-13). Pastors are God's representatives to His people who perform His work; therefore, they must be held in high regard and love. This esteem is not to be based on personality or charm but on the fact the pastor is God's anointed man filling a divinely appointed position.

Paul also teaches in this passage that members within the body must submit to pastoral authority so that "peace" prevails within the church (verse 14). All godly pastors are to be honored, but some are "worthy of double honour" (1 Timothy 5:17).

Qualifications for a pastor are set forth in 1 Timothy 3:1-7 and are eloquently reflected by William Barclay:

> The picture of the shepherd is indelibly written on the New Testament. He was the man who cared for the flock and led the sheep into safe places; he was the man who sought the sheep when they wandered away and, if need be, died to save them. The shepherd of the flock of God is the man who bears God's people on his heart, who feeds them with the truth, who seeks them when they stray away, and who defends them from all that would hurt their faith.[201]

Deacon—1 Timothy 3:8-13 and Acts 6:1-7

The role of the deacon is to assist in spiritual and temporal matters so as to grant the pastor quality time in prayer and ministry of the Word. Note the order of importance cited in this text for the pastor: prayer first, then preaching.

The term *deacon* comes from the Greek word *diakonos* ("servant" or "minister"). Taking into account its use in a range of scriptures, it means:

> caring for those in prison (Matthew 25:44), serving tables (meeting physical needs, Acts 6:2), teaching the Word of God (Acts 6:4), giving money to meet others' needs (2 Corinthians 9:1), and all service offered by Christians to others to build them up in faith (1 Corinthians 12:5; Ephesians 4:12).[202]

There is no scripture that suggests deacons are given authority over the pastor or power to "rule" the church.

Qualifications for a deacon are set forth in 1 Timothy 3:8-13. Deacons are to manifest the following eight characteristics:

(1) Serious-minded men in the faith;
(2) Not double-tongued, but men who do not vacillate in what they tell various people;
(3) Not given to much wine;
(4) Not dishonest and do not use the office of deacon for financial gain;
(5) Holding the mystery of the faith in a pure conscience: they practice what they proclaim;
(6) Blameless: men who have been tested and found worthy to hold the office;
(7) Men whose wife is faithful in all things (reliable) and does not gossip;
(8) The husband of one wife—men who manage their households well.

The deacon is to meet the same requirements as the pastor except for ability to teach the Word (1 Timothy 3:2).

Evangelist in the Church at Large (Ephesians 4:11 -12)

Christ instituted the office of evangelist at the same time He did that of the pastor (Ephesians 4:11). The office of evangelist was established by our ascending Lord to plant churches, partner with churches in evangelism, pursue souls, preach the Gospel, and perfect ("equip") the saints. This office has not been deleted and the evangelist's call has not been rescinded by Christ. And it will not be "til we all come in the unity of the faith, and of the knowledge of the Son of God, unto a perfect man, unto the measure of the stature of the fullness of Christ" (Ephesians 4:13).

Spurgeon is clear about the critical part evangelists play in the health of the body of Christ:

> From our ascended Lord come all true evangelists; these are they who preach the gospel in divers places, and find it the power of God unto salvation; they are founders of churches, breakers of new soil, men of a missionary spirit, who build not on other men's foundations, but dig out for themselves. We need many such deliverers of the good news where as yet the message has not been heard. I scarcely know of any greater blessing to the church than the sending forth of earnest, indefatigable, anointed men of God, taught of the Lord to be winners of souls.[203]

> *"The calling of evangelist is one of the great gifts that God has given to the church, and is as important as the seminary professor, or church pastor....A great need in the church today is to recognize and dignify the gift of the evangelist."*[204]
> —Billy Graham

The evangelist:

- is a traveling preacher, divinely set aside, gifted, and authorized by God to proclaim the message of the Cross to the unsaved (literally one who announces the Good News);
- is set apart by Christ for the building up of the church numerically;
- is not restricted to one church but serves the church of Christ at large, unlike the pastoral office;
- receives his livelihood (financial support) by faith; to be provided by the churches, camps, and conferences he serves—and by Christians at large;
- lives an uncommon life, moving about constantly from city to city;
- is often separated from family and friends, sleeps in various places, eats irregularly, lives with uncertainty about how bills and living needs will be supplied, and serves people who at times are critical of his work.

> *"Evangelists are a gift of Christ to the churches and are not to be despised, rejected, neglected, or unjustly criticized. Their work is just as important in its relationship to the whole program of Christ as the work of other gifts...."*[205]
> —Faris Whitsell

THE UNITED FUNCTION OF THE PASTORAL AND EVANGELIST OFFICES

Pastors and evangelists support each other. Evangelists are primarily "obstetricians," and pastors are "pediatricians." Evangelists are harvest men given to the church—gifted in the spiritual birthing of the unsaved—while pastors nurture the newly re-born, edifying the body of Christ (1 Corinthians 3:4–9). Wayne Barber explains this division of labor:

> So you have your evangelists, then you have your pastor/teachers. These are the Master's men. Instead of gifts bestowed upon men, we have got gifted men bestowed upon the church. This is so the church can begin to grow and come into the stature of the fullness of Christ. It is required to be equipped, so He gives the equippers to the church.[206]

A BIBLICAL PICTURE OF THE EVANGELIST

Acts 21:8 and 8:26-40 present a picture of the biblical evangelist Philip who illustrates the characteristics of an evangelist:

- The *motive* of the evangelist is the divine call placed on his life (8:26, Ephesians 4:11). He is thrust into the work of evangelism by the Holy Spirit and is passionate about doing it. The evangelist has no discretionary power to alter this call—he must simply obey it.
- The *message* of the evangelist is "Jesus Christ and Him crucified" (8:35).
- The *method* of the evangelist is simply readiness to go and tell the gospel story compassionately to all people regardless of place, people, or price (8:27, 40). The evangelist knows how to present Christ to the unsaved tactfully but also is gifted by God to draw the net, bringing the lost to a decision whether privately or in public services (8:37). The evangelist's task is to make the presentation of the gospel crystal clear in America and beyond so all can understand.

THE EVANGELIST AND REVIVAL

Revivals have long been a successful tool for evangelism and the mainstay for the evangelist financially. With revival meetings in decline, the church must utilize evangelists for other ministries and embrace them financially, or they may be forced out of their work, to the serious detriment of the Kingdom.

> *"It is a sin of commission to reject the divine office of the evangelist: a sin of omission to ignore the office; and a sin of transgression to abuse the office."*[207]
>
> —Don Womack

Faris Whitsell echoes the same idea:

> Conclude, then, that Christ still grants the evangelistic gift to chosen men. Churches should recognize and use evangelists. If so-called evangelists have been unworthy of the title that does not mean that evangelists as a class have been discredited.[208]

GROWING IN KNOWLEDGE, LIVING BY FAITH

UNIT 11

REVIEW

(1) What is the primary role of the pastor? _____ The deacon? _____

(2) In what ways is the evangelist a gift to the church by the ascended Lord? _____

(3) Has the office of evangelist ceased? _____ What about apostle? _____
Prophet? _____

(4) How does the biblical evangelist Philip reflect the general characteristics of an evangelist? _____

(5) According to 1 Timothy 3, what is the one requirement for pastor that differs from the requirements for deacon? _____

MENTORING

Paul instructs older women in the church to mentor the young women in regard to seven matters (Titus 2:2-5). The older men in the church have an equal responsibility to mentor the young men. Barnabas took Paul, for instance, under his wing while Paul was just a babe in Christ, and developed him in the things of Christ:

> But Barnabas took him [Paul] and brought him to the apostles, and declared unto them how he had seen the Lord in the way, and that he had spoken to him, and how he had preached boldly at Damascus in the name of Jesus. (Acts 9:27)

The words "took him" literally mean that Barnabas physically held on to Paul to help him. The Apostle Paul would not have become what he was for God had it not been for Barnabas's mentorship in his early life.

The failure of the spiritually mature to coach growing believers, church leaders, and preacher-boys is the great weakness of the modern church movement. Yet the ministry of mentoring (spiritual coaching) is the greatest work that can be done outside of soulwinning. Mentoring is the ministry of taking younger men or women under protective and provisional wings to edify, educate, embolden, emancipate, enlighten, establish, excite, and equip in spiritual matters.

The work of mentoring, though joyful, is extremely demanding and occasionally disappointing. It requires time, resources, sacrifice, devotion, and prayers. Robert E. Coleman describes the challenge:

> What perhaps is the most difficult part of the whole process of training is that we must anticipate their problems and prepare them for what they will face. This is terribly hard to do and can become exasperating. It means that we can seldom put them out of our mind. Even when we are in our private meditations and study, our disciples will be in our prayers and dreams. Would a parent who loves his children want it any other way? We have to accept the burden of their immaturity until such time as they can do it for themselves.[209]

An excellent pattern for mentoring is found in the relationship of the Apostle Paul to Timothy (2 Timothy 1-3). Paul models seven key components of effective mentoring:

(1) *Conviction* (1:11). The blind cannot lead the blind. It is imperative the mentor be a person of biblical soundness, separation, and surrender.
(2) *Confirmation* (1:5-6). The infusion of confidence and certainty regarding salvation and the ministry call by the mentor is essential. The coach has to help the disciple believe in him- or herself.
(3) *Cultivation* (1:13; 3:14). This requires imparting God's Word to the soul and watering until it sprouts. The mentor must constantly sow sound biblical doctrine and teaching into the disciple. The spiritual coach must be as a "barking dog" to the disciple, continuously warning of potential "snares," heresy, and soul neglect.
(4) *Correction* (1:7). The mentor must confront moral and spiritual faults and weaknesses (Galatians 6:1). Mentors hold their disciples accountable—morally, ethically, and spiritually.
(5) *Commendation* (1:3). The display of approval in lessons learned and battles won encourages the disciple to press forward. Imagine how Timothy's heart must have raced in hearing that a spiritual giant like Paul thanked God for him and believed in him. Give praise when praise is due.
(6) *Clarification* (2:16-19). The mentor's task is to clear up any misunderstanding or misinterpretation regarding Scripture or personal decisions made.
(7) *Compulsion* (1:14; 2:3; 2:22; 3:14; 4:1-5). The spiritual coach must compel, incite, and motivate the disciple to keep a tight grip on "that good thing (Gospel) which was committed unto them by the Holy Ghost" (1:14). The disciple must be taught patience and persistence, and must see his or her potential despite suffering, persecution, failure, or discouragement. Mentors must exhort disciples never to quit or give up on the faith or divine call.

Solomon said, "Iron sharpeneth iron" (Proverbs 27:17). The Lord counts on spiritually mature believers to sharpen young Christians in doctrine, devotion, and duty until they then can do the same for someone else. Young Christians—and anyone going into ministry—should seek out a godly person to be a spiritual coach. (Note: Mentors and disciples should always be of the same sex.) The spiritually mature must now, more than ever, invest in new believers and young ministers, allowing rivers of spiritual knowledge and experience to flow into and through them.

Billy Graham was once asked what his strategy would be if he were the pastor of a large church in a major city. The evangelist replied:

> I think one of the first things I would do would be to get a small group of eight, or ten, or twelve men around me that would meet a few hours a week and pay the price! It would cost them something in time and effort. I would share everything I have, over a period of years. Then I would actually have twelve ministers among the laymen who in turn could take eight or ten or twelve more and teach them.... Christ, I think, set the pattern. He spent most of His time with twelve men. He didn't spend it with the great crowd. In fact, every time He had a great crowd it seems to me that there weren't too many results. The great results, it seems to me, came in his personal interview and in the time He spent with His twelve.[210]

GROWING IN KNOWLEDGE, LIVING BY FAITH
UNIT 11

THE "HOW TO'S" OF CHURCH MEMBERSHIP

A believer asked a friend during the sermon invitation, "Are you ready to join the church?" The friend replied, "I don't know how."

So how does someone unite with the church?

At the conclusion of a church worship service, an invitation to respond to the message is extended. At this point, a person may approach the pastor to indicate his or her desire to join the church. Some churches provide additional ways to become a member of their fellowship.

THE INVITATION

The invitation at the climax of a sermon is customary in most Baptist churches. Although some question its purpose and criticize its practice and some see it merely as an addendum to the sermon—a time to prepare to exit the sanctuary—I believe it is a vital part of the sermon. Speaking to evangelists from around the world at Amsterdam '83, Billy Graham posed the question, "Is it valid or legitimate to extend an invitation for people to come to Christ?" Then he thundered his own, one-word answer: "Yes!"[211]

Stressing the importance of the invitation, C. E. Matthews declared:

> When the service is concluded and the congregation stands for the invitation, the moment has struck for the consummation of everything that has been done in the name of the Lord up to that hour for that one thing. All the work in preparation—the census, the contacts in visitation, the publicity, the prayer meetings, money contributed, everything—was for that invitation. All that has transpired in that particular service—the sermon, the praying, the music, the time spent by the congregation in worship—everything has been done to make ready for that invitation.[212]

Throughout Scripture, you'll find invitation after invitation. God extended the first invitation to Adam and Eve after their sin when he cried out to them "Where art thou?" (Genesis 3:9). Moses issued an invitation at the base of Sinai following his sermon to the multitude of people: "Who is on the Lord's side, let him come unto me" (Exodus 32:26). Joshua invited the Israelites: "Choose you this day whom you will serve" (Joshua 24:15). Jesus presented an invitation to Simon and Andrew when He said, "Come ye after me, and I will make you to become fishers of men" (Mark 1:17). Jesus issued a clear invitation in Revelation 3:20: "Behold I stand at the door and knock: if any man hear my voice and open the door I will come to him."

THE CHRISTIAN'S ROLE IN THE INVITATION

Largely due to lack of instruction, many church members are clueless about their responsibility during the invitation. I spoke about this once at a conference after which many in the audience told me, "I never heard a sermon on the invitation until tonight." C. E. Matthews shared the confession of a church member who, after hearing a talk about the invitation, lamented:

Pastor, I never realized how I had failed in my responsibility when an invitation was given in the service. I have just been awakened to a thing that I have never known before, and that is the tremendous burden that must be on the heart of a preacher when he is making his appeal and trying to persuade people to accept Christ as Savior. I am ashamed of myself. When you begin the invitation, I have been guilty of powdering my face and applying lipstick without any thought of what I was doing. I have asked God to forgive me, and I am asking you to forgive me and to pray for me that I will share with you and others the responsibility of helping people decide for Christ during the invitation.[213]

SO WHAT SHOULD YOU AS A CHRISTIAN DO DURING THE INVITATION?

It is a time for *reflection* upon the Word of God spoken and the challenges presented.

The invitation is a time for *introspection* with questions like: "What am I being asked to do?" or "Is this something I need to do?"

It is a time for *deliberation* over the action, commitment that one needs to make: "Is this something I am willing to do?"

The invitation is a time for *resolution*: "Will I make this commitment here and now?"

The invitation is a time for *application*: "I will do it."

Reflection, inspection, deliberation, and resolution lead to decision. The "I will do it" of application. At this point, the person publicly reveals his or her commitment by walking the aisle to the minister.

The invitation is also a time for *intercession*. Believers ought to pray for the unsaved to respond once their own personal decisions are settled.

Giving an invitation at the conclusion of his sermon, Billy Graham expresses the gravity of the moment: "I ask that no one leave. This is the real moment for which we are here."[214]

The serious nature of the invitation requires an attitude of reverence, receptivity, and response. Distractions such as departing the worship room, talking, or readying to leave the service while the invitation is in progress must be avoided. My book, *The Evangelistic Invitation 101,* addresses this subject in depth (available at www.frankshivers.com).

REVIEW

(1) Who was the Apostle Paul's mentor? _____

(2) What are the seven characteristics of effective mentoring? _____

(3) List some of the invitations recorded in Scripture. _____

(4) What are five things everyone—believers and non-believers alike—should do during the invitation? _____

GROWING IN KNOWLEDGE, LIVING BY FAITH
UNIT 11

> # NEGLECT NOT: THE SANCTUARY
>
> *"Do not forsake the assembling of yourselves together as the manner of some is, but exhort one another; and so much the more as ye see the day approaching."*
>
> —Hebrews 10:25
>
> Don't abandon or desert the church but stay integrally involved. Your life or ministry will not count for much outside the church. In times of spiritual coldness and indifference, it is especially important to neglect not attending church. God continually uses the church to reach and reclaim His erring children.

REFLECT—*Consider What This Means*

(1) Are you acting like a "dog" in your Christian walk, or have you accepted your need as a "sheep" to be part of a flock? _____

(2) If you are a pastor or deacon, how do you measure up to the qualifications outlined in 1 Timothy 3? _____

(3) Read Titus 2:2-5, and identify the seven matters in which older women are to mentor younger women. _____

(4) What is your personal role during the sermon's invitation? _____

RESPOND—*What Will You Do with What You Know?*

(1) Have you been attending a church but, for some reason, are reluctant to join? If it is a biblically sound church, you probably need to commit yourself. Speak to your pastor about it, and respond to the invitation the next time you have a chance.
(2) Is God calling you to an office in the church—pastor, deacon, or evangelist? _____ If you've never opened yourself to the possibility, start now to pray that God will make clear what you should do—and when.
(3) Pray that "the Lord of the harvest" will raise up more evangelists, that He will open "doors of utterance" for evangelists, and that the needs of evangelists will be supplied "according to the riches of God in Christ Jesus."
(4) You may need a mentor, or you may be ready to become a mentor for someone. Pray daily for the next week about which applies to you. Then take action on whichever direction God leads you.
(5) Read *The Evangelistic Invitation 101*.

UNIT 12

UNDERSTANDING GOD'S WILL

"A preacher really has a tough time, doesn't he?" I recall telling my best friend after a minister's talk at a Key Club meeting. I was a junior at Lower Richland High School, and something special stirred in my heart that day.

My friend responded to the question I posed, "He sure does, why?" His eyes widened. "You're not thinking about becoming one are you?"

That same night my mother called me aside and asked if I was considering the ministry. She mentioned that many people at our church were wondering the same thing. Needless to say, I was considering that very thing, and God used her and the inquiry of other saints to confirm my call.

Although God issued my call more than 45 years ago, it's just as fresh and real as when I was sixteen. God is still in the business of calling believers of various ages into vocational Christian service as He did me. Perhaps He is calling you.

In this study, we'll clarify the earmarks of a call into vocational ministry. Even if you determine that's not the call on your life, the principles of discerning God's will apply to any decision you'll make in life. The crucial point is to submit everything to the authority of God's will for you.

VOCATIONAL CHRISTIAN SERVICE

The shortage of missionaries, pastors, evangelists, children's and youth ministers, and musicians and music leaders is not due to a lack of calling on God's part. It is due either to ignorance about the potential or an unwillingness to hear or respond.

God will call clearly and unmistakably, taking steps to insure the right man receives the right call. He called Jonah by name, invoked his father's name, and even cited the place where they lived (Jonah 1:1). God removed from Jonah's mind any doubt about the validity or specificity of the call (Jonah 1:2). This is God's pattern for everyone to whom He extends a call to Christian vocation.

> *Do not ask whether something is possible; ask whether it is right, and God will enable you to do it.*[215]
>
> —William Booth

In Isaiah 6:8, God asked Isaiah the key question for any ministry or mission: "Whom shall I send? And who will go for me?" About how to apply this question personally, the great church leader and theologian John Wesley once wrote George Whitefield asking, "What, Mr. Whitefield, if thou art that man?"[216] Whitefield went on to shake a continent for God.

God asks every Christian the same question: "What if thou art that man?" What if God is calling you to missions, the pastorate, evangelism, student ministry, or music ministry? Each of us should stand ready to respond with Isaiah, Whitefield, and millions of others: "Here am I. Send me, send me."

> *"All giants have been weak men and women who did great things for God because they reckoned on His power and presence to be with them."* [217]
>
> —Hudson Taylor

C.H. Spurgeon extols the richness of the beckoning of God to serve:

> The call of Christ's servants comes from above. Jesus stands on the mountain, evermore above the world in holiness, earnestness, love and power. Those whom he calls must go up the mountain to him, they must seek to rise to his level by living in constant communion with him. They may not be able to mount to classic honours, or attain scholastic eminence, but they must like Moses go up into the mount of God and have familiar intercourse with the unseen God, or they will never be fitted to proclaim the gospel of peace. [218]

What an honor and privilege to be "called out" by God for vocational ministry. Indeed, as another has said, "If God calls you into the ministry, don't stoop to be a President or a King." According to Christ, the Church at large is to pray for an increase of full-time servants:

> The harvest truly *is* plenteous, but the labourers *are* few; pray ye therefore the Lord of the harvest, that he will send forth labourers into his harvest. (Matthew 9:37-38)

Regardless of location or circumstance, the call to vocational Christian ministry is for life or until Christ withdraws it.

Hear what Paul declares in Ephesians 2:10, a remarkable passage regarding God's purpose and call for the believer. Paul says we are "created in Christ Jesus unto good works, which God hath before ordained that we should walk in them." Let's unpack what this teaches:

> **WORD WISDOM: SPIRITUAL GIFTS**
>
> Gifts bestowed to believers by the Holy Spirit at conversion that vary from believer to believer (*Romans 12:6-8; 1 Corinthians 12:8-10; 12:28; 12:29-30*).

- "Created in Christ Jesus" means Christians have new life through the new birth in Christ Jesus;
- "Unto good works" suggests that every believer is saved to engage in a life of service;
- "Which God hath before ordained" indicates God designed this life of service in ages past;
- "That we should walk in them" means this plan of service is knowable and doable.

All through this great text runs the pivotal theme that *God has a plan for every life in Christ Jesus*. Every Christian is called to serve God in a general sense while some are called to serve Him in a specific sense as vocational servants.

UNDERSTANDING GOD'S WILL
UNIT 12

In Ephesians 4:11-12, Paul lists the ways God uses His people:

> And he gave some, apostles; and some, prophets; and some, evangelists; and some, pastors and teachers; For the perfecting of the saints, for the work of the ministry, for the edifying of the body of Christ.

So how can a believer know if God is extending a call into full-time Christian service? It's easy to be puzzled over this thing we designate as a "call":

- How does it come?
- How do you know when it comes?
- When does it come?
- How do you say "Yes" to it when it comes?

I assure you God's will is not vague or hidden but readily knowable. And discovering His will for your life is pivotal to having maximum usefulness, happiness, and peace in life. God wants us to know His plans for us:

> See then that you walk circumspectly, not as fools but as wise, redeeming the time, because the days are evil. Therefore do not be unwise, but understand what the will of the Lord is."
> (Ephesians 5:15–17)

We should not be like Lewis Carroll's *Alice in Wonderland*. When she asked the cat for directions, the cat, in turn asked her, "Where do you want to go?" She replied, "It doesn't matter." To which the cat offered the logical response: "Then it doesn't matter which way you go."

For the Christian, direction in life *does* matter—at least it ought to. God does have a plan, so it matters enormously which way you go.

REVIEW

(1) The principles of discerning a call to vocational Christian service can be applied to any of life's decisions.   ❏ True   ❏ False

(2) How does Jonah 1:1 reinforce the idea that God's call will be specific? _____

(3) Like Isaiah, what should our response be to God's question, "Whom shall I send?" _____

(4) According to Hudson Taylor, how do weak men become giants for God? _____

(5) How long does the call to Christian service last? _____
(6) What is the central theme of Ephesians 2:10? _____

GROWING IN KNOWLEDGE, LIVING BY FAITH
UNIT 12

SIGNS OF THE CALL

When you're on a trip, road signs help you know where to go. Similarly, God posts signs along the road of life to guide His children. In the pages that follow, I've used road signs as an analogy to the way God gives Divine direction for His children. As Scripture promises:

• The Lord is good and does what is right; he shows the proper path to those who go astray. He leads the humble in doing right, teaching them his way. The Lord leads with unfailing love and faithfulness to all who keep his covenant and obey his demands (Psalm 25:8-10, NLT).

• The God of our fathers has chosen you that you should know His will, and see the Just One, and hear the voice of His mouth (Acts 22:14).

• "For I know the plans I have for you," declares the Lord, "plans to prosper you and not to harm you, plans to give you hope and a future (Jeremiah 29:11)."

YIELD

Knowledge of God's will begins with a yielded heart. God will not reveal His plan until you are willing to know it *and* do what He says. So the first step in discerning the call of God is to have a heart submissive and open to whatever God desires. Yieldedness is the foundation of serving God. As Paul bids the Christians in Rome:

I beseech you therefore, brethren, by the mercies of God, that you present your bodies a living sacrifice, holy, acceptable to God, which is your reasonable service. And do not be conformed to this world, but be transformed by the renewing of your mind, that you may prove what is that good and acceptable and perfect will of God (Romans 12: 1-2).

Obedience is the opener of eyes.[219]
—George McDonald

It is not enough to be merely curious about what God might want of us. That sort of curiosity will never be satisfied. God shares only with those who are committed to doing whatever He directs. God reveals His will to you not for your thoughtful consideration but for your wholehearted submission.

To know the will of God, we need an open Bible and an open map.[220]

— William Carey, pioneer missionary to India

> **WORD WISDOM: HYPOCRISY**
>
> The act of preaching or declaring one thing regarding belief and conduct while practicing another intentionally; "mask wearing" as in theatrical performances, leading others to believe a person is someone he is not. Jesus strongly condemns hypocrisy in the church (*Luke 6:42; Matthew 15:7-8*). D. L. Moody called hypocrisy "talking cream and living skim milk."[221]

UNDERSTANDING GOD'S WILL
UNIT 12

MEN AT WORK

When Abraham's servant sought a wife for Isaac, God led him to Rebekah. Upon meeting her, the servant explained himself to Rebekah, saying, "I being in the way, the Lord led me" (Genesis 24:27). It is essential that you spend time "in the way"—in obedience and intimate communion with God—if you want to be led by God.

When your heart soars at the right altitude with God, it can hear His voice, even when you're not specifically looking for His call. That was my experience. As a junior in high school, I had never once pondered the possibility of a call to ministry, but because of my spiritual walk, I heard God when He invited me to join Him in His work. Keep stoking the fire for God in your soul so that when He speaks, you will hear. The more you work at knowing God intimately and loving Him passionately the easier it will be for you to recognize His voice. Max Lucado expands on this truth:

> We learn God's will by spending time in his presence. The key to knowing God's heart is having a relationship with him. A personal relationship. God will speak to you differently than he will speak to others. Just because God spoke to Moses through a burning bush, that doesn't mean we should all sit next to a bush waiting for God to speak. God used a fish to convict Jonah. Does that mean we should have worship services at Sea World? No. God reveals his heart personally to each person. For that reason, your walk with God is essential. His heart is not seen in an occasional chat or weekly visit. We learn his will as we take up residence in his house every single day. Walk with him long enough and you come to know his heart."[222]

Intimacy with the Almighty that leads to knowledge of His will is conditioned not only upon communion with Him but holiness of conduct: "The pure in heart shall see God (Matthew 5:8)." A foundational prayer in seeking God's will is confession and petition for cleansing: "Search me, O God, and know my heart; Try me, and know my thoughts; And see if there is any wicked way in me, And lead me in the way everlasting (Psalm 139:23-24)."

> "The will of God is not like a magic package let down from heaven by a string...the will of God is far more like a scroll that unrolls every day...the will of God is something to be discerned and lived out every day of our lives. It is not something to be grasped as a package once for all. In other words, God will guide you and me today, and tomorrow, and the next day and the day after that. One day at a time. Our call, then, is to follow the Lord Jesus Christ, to walk with him in a daily close relationship. It is first of all *being* not *doing*."[223]
>
> —Paul Little

GROWING IN KNOWLEDGE, LIVING BY FAITH
UNIT 12

REVIEW

(1) What does Romans 12:1-2 say are the first five essentials in knowing the perfect will of God? _____

(2) Does God want you to know His will for your life? _____ What must your attitude be in order to hear what He has to say? _____

(3) What does it mean to be "in the way" with the Lord? _____

(4) What does Max Lucado say is required to learn God's will? _____

(5) What besides communion with God is required to know His will? _____

TELEPHONE SIGN

Knock on heaven's door—prayer is the ignition key to fire up the process of finding God's will. Prayer gives God a green light, the right of way to speak to you about His plan. It's your way of placing a call to God.

Wisdom and discernment are acquired through prayer: "But if any of you needs wisdom, you should ask God for it. He is generous to everyone and will give you wisdom without criticizing you (James 1:5 NCV)." In other words, James says that the believer who wants to know God's will should go to Him saying, "God, I do want to fulfill your plan for my life, but I need divine wisdom to know that plan and how to engage it." We cannot expect God to give the illumination we need if we don't ask Him for it. Solomon, too, insisted that believers rely wholly on insights from God:

> Trust the Lord with all your heart, and don't depend on your own understanding. Remember the LORD in all you do, and he will give you success. Don't depend on your own wisdom. Respect the Lord and refuse to do wrong (Proverbs 3:5-7, NCV).

God promises over and over to answer our prayers to know Him:

> • "Ask, and God will give to you. Search, and you will find. Knock, and the door will open for you. Yes, everyone who asks will receive. Everyone who searches will find. And everyone who knocks will have the door opened (Matthew 7:7-8, NCV)."

> • "Call unto me, and I will answer thee, and show thee great and mighty things, which thou knowest not (Jeremiah 33:3)."

Along with asking for God's wisdom, we must set aside our personal preferences and our own plans. John Wesley said, "I found that the chief purpose in determining the will of God is to get my will in an unprejudiced state about the issue at hand. Then, when my will is unprejudiced, I find that God suggests reason to my mind concerning the proper course."[224] Prayer alone can enable this to be done.

If you are patient by waiting before God in prayer for His divine communication, clarification, and confirmation, He will reveal what you seek. To help focus your heart, try praying this straightforward Psalm:

> Show me thy ways, O LORD; teach me thy paths. Lead me in thy truth, and teach me: for thou art the God of my salvation; on thee do I wait all the day (Psalm 25:4-5).

TURN HEADLIGHTS ON

What will light the way ahead for you? Psalm 19:8 answers frankly, "The statutes of the LORD are right, rejoicing the heart: the commandment of the LORD is pure, enlightening the eyes." Holy Scripture transmits light (divine knowledge) to the soul. David says "More to be desired are they than gold, yea than much fine gold: sweeter also than honey and the honeycomb" (Psalm 19:10). Don't live in the dark or make decisions in the dark. Turn on the headlights of God's Word for illumination: "Thy Word O Lord is a lamp unto my feet, a light unto my path" (Psalm 119:105).

> *He will never call you to do a work His Word denounces.*

ACCELERATION LANE

A sense of urgent, persistent compulsion is one of the marks of an authentic call. Do you burn with a compulsion to minister as a pastor, evangelist, missionary, or church planter? Never fear that God will call you to do a service that is distasteful. He always gives with the task the desire to do it. If you are walking closely with God, then it is legitimate to ask yourself, "Is this something I want to do now?" God will use a submitted heart's desire to speak to you.

> The voice of the *Baptist Hour* (for 18 years), Hershel Hobbs, advised, God calls all Christians to serve Him. But in a special way, He calls some into distinctly Christian vocations. A preacher should not choose the ministry but should be chosen for it. Yet so deeply personal and spiritual is the call that no preacher can explain his call to another. But a preacher knows he is called. Otherwise he should not try to fill this role.[225]
> —Richard Allen Bodey

CAR POOL

God uses His people to endorse those whom He calls. For me, my mother and the church confirmed my call. Consult with people you know who are deeply spiritual, who possess great discernment, and who will be candid in their advice to you.

> *Considerable weight is to be given to the judgment of men and women who live near to God, and in most instances their verdict will not be a mistaken one.*[226]
>
> —C. H. Spurgeon

GROWING IN KNOWLEDGE, LIVING BY FAITH
UNIT 12

Remember Samuel's experience when he was about 12 years old? He was awakened one night by a voice calling, "Samuel, Samuel." But he was too spiritually immature to know it was God. Eli, though, a mature believer, told him to say upon hearing the voice again, "Speak Lord, for thy servant heareth (1 Samuel 3:10)."

Many identify with Samuel: God is calling but they do not recognize His voice and need someone else to clarify the heavenly call. So when a precious saint speaks of the possibility of God's call on your life, take it seriously and make inquiry of the Lord.

God also uses His people to confirm His call. Once you think you know the will of God, ask a spiritually mature brother or sister if they see evidence of such a call upon your life. Do those who know you best in the church encourage you to pursue it? If so, God may well be making His will known. Finally, Christians are not only to confirm God's call (or not) but to intercede for those seeking to know God's will. Paul did this for the believers to whom he ministered:

> For this reason we also, since the day we heard it, do not cease to pray for you, and to ask that you may be filled with the knowledge of His will in all wisdom and spiritual understanding (Colossians 1:9).

REVIEW

(1) What does James 1:5 say you should ask for in knowing God's will? _____
(2) Along with asking for God's wisdom, you must set aside your _____ and your _____.
(3) What lights your path? _____
(4) If you're walking closely with God, the answer to what question can help you discern God's will? _____
(5) How does the "Car Pool" sign reflect the way God can make His will known? _____

DO NOT ENTER

The possession or absence of spiritual gifts can help discern God's will. For example, if you cannot sing, most likely God is not calling you to be a vocal musician. On the other hand, if you feel comfortable speaking before people, God may be calling you into the preaching ministry.

While I was in seminary, several friends wrestled with clarification of their call to music or preaching ministry. This was never a problem with me, however, due to my singing ability (I have none). As with me and singing, there are some calls the believer can pretty much rule out from the get-go. Referring to this kind of "sanctified common sense," Adrian Rogers stated, "Ninety percent of God's will is found between your ears."[227]

God always equips with the necessary gifts to accomplish the work assigned, as He did with Moses, for instance. God's call will take advantage of the strengths He has bestowed on you. A person

UNDERSTANDING GOD'S WILL
UNIT 12

operating within the arena of his chief giftedness will be the most successful. Therefore, your giftedness is a solid indicator of the type of service God is calling you to undertake. God fits the man with the task for which he is the most qualified.

God also uses spiritual markers. Genesis 13:3-4 says of Abraham:

> He went on his journeys from the Negev as far as Bethel, to the place where his tent had been at the beginning, between Bethel and Ai, to the place of the altar which he had made there formerly; and there Abram called on the name of the LORD.

After living in Egypt, Abraham returned to the place where he had previously called upon the name of the Lord. This was a spiritual marker in his life.

> **WORD WISDOM: TRIBULATION**
>
> (1) The oppression and persecution believers confront in living for Christ (*2 Thessalonians 3:4*).
> (2) The Great Tribulation is a seven-year period of suffering and persecution under the reign of the Antichrist that follows the rapture of the church (*Revelation 7:14; Matthew 24:21-22; 2 Thessalonians 2:8-9*).

Spiritual markers can be places or reference points which identify a transition, decision, or direction when God clearly gave guidance.[228] In looking at these markers, a person can readily see the direction God is moving his or her life. These markers are important in understanding God's guidance. When you encounter a new marker along the way (a call to ministry, for example), it is helpful to look at the previous markers you've encountered. If they all seem to point the same way, then you are most likely moving in the right direction.

FOOD AND LODGING

We all prefer one food over another. You can apply this "principle" appetite to Christian service. What would you rather do more than anything else in the world? What would give you the greatest degree of emotional and spiritual satisfaction? If you are walking in deep devotion with the Lord, the answers to these questions can be an indicator of God's direction for your life.

REVIEW

(1) How can giftedness help you discern God's will? _____

(2) What is a spiritual marker? _____
(3) If your spiritual markers line up, then you are most likely moving in the _____.

(4) How does your spiritual appetite help to reveal God's will? _____

TURN FOG LIGHTS ON

The Quakers call the impression of the Holy Spirit in one's heart the "inner light." This light makes known what is God's good and perfect will. Scripture explains, "For as many as are led by the Spirit of God, they are the sons of God (Romans 8:14)." The impression of the Holy Spirit will clarify and cement God's call. Holy Spirit "fog lights" will open your understanding and give peace about the direction to go. Pay attention to these spiritual impressions or nudges.

A. W. Pink clarifies how to hear the inner voice of God:

> There is a safe and sure criterion by which the Christian may gauge his inner impulses, and ascertain whether they proceed from his own restless spirit, an evil spirit or the Spirit of God. That criterion is the written Word of God, and by it all must be measured. The Holy Spirit never prompts anyone to act contrary to the Scriptures. How could He, when He is the Author of them! His promptings are always unto obedience to the precepts of Holy Writ. Therefore, when a man who has not been distinctly called, separated, and qualified by God to be a minister of His Word undertakes to "preach," no matter how strong the impulse, it proceeds not from the Holy Spirit.[229]

> *'I will guide thee with mine eye (Psalm 32:8). As servants take their cue from the master's eye, and a nod or a wink is all that they require, so should we obey the slightest hints of our Master, not needing thunderbolts to startle our incorrigible sluggishness, but being controlled by whispers and love-touches.*[230]
> —C. H. Spurgeon

WEIGH STATION AHEAD

In Luke 14:27-30, Jesus tells the story of a king weighing his options before going into battle. His point is that a believer should seriously consider the cost of a decision before proceeding. This is never truer than with regard to a decision about full-time Christian service. The key preparatory questions are:

- What will submission to God's call cost me, my family and friends?
- Am I willing to pay that price to obey God?

Don't simply make a flippant decision saying "I will go" without counting the cost. The "drop-out" rate among pastors is shocking—1600 every month. And less than half of current seminary students will be in the ministry five years from now. Failure to count the cost is the problem.

The time to assess what ministry will require is before you say "Yes." But you can rely on God to enable you to overcome every obstacle, meet every challenge, and withstand every hardship you'll face in fulfilling the call. If you walk like Abraham in unflinching faith, God will walk with you on your journey and will fulfill through you His sovereign plan:

UNDERSTANDING GOD'S WILL
UNIT 12

It was by faith that Abraham obeyed when God called him to leave home and go to another land that God would give him as his inheritance. He went without knowing where he was going (Hebrews 11:8, NLT).

He is no fool who gives up what he cannot keep to gain that which he cannot lose.[231]

— Jim Eliot, missionary martyr who lost his life in the 1950's trying to reach the Auca Indians of Ecuador

THE ROAD MAP

God chooses, the Holy Spirit confirms, and man submits. Running from the call, as Jonah did, does not nullify the call (Jonah 1:1-3), "for the gifts and the call of God are irrevocable" (Romans 11:29). Nor is it without consequence. Jonah paid for his disobedience. And so will anyone else who refuses God.

To stay here and disobey God—I can't afford to take the consequence. I would rather go and obey God than to stay here and know that I disobeyed.[232]

—Amanda Berry Smith

If you are someone chosen to carry His message vocationally, then count it all joy and the highest of honors. Refuse to turn back or give up, regardless of cost or consequence. Nothing is more important than expending your life doing what God designed.

The will of God—nothing less, nothing more, nothing else.[233]

—F. E. Marsh

In the words of B. B. McKinney's song:

"Take up thy cross and follow Me," I heard my Master say;
"I gave My life to ransom thee, Surrender your all today."
Wherever He leads I'll go, Wherever He leads I'll go,
I'll follow my Christ who loves me so, Wherever He leads I'll go.

My heart, my life, my all I bring To Christ who loves me so;
he is my Master, Lord, and King, Wherever He leads I'll go.
Wherever He leads I'll go, Wherever He leads I'll go,
I'll follow my Christ who loves me so, Wherever He leads I'll go."[234]

J. H. JOWETT ON THE CALL TO CHRISTIAN MINISTRY

And so we cannot tell how the call will come to us, what will be the manner of its coming. It may be that the divine constraint will be as soft as a glance: "I will guide thee with Mine eye." It may be that we can scarcely describe the guidance, it is so shy and quiet and unobtrusive. Or it may be that the constraint will seize us as with a strong and invisible grip, as though we were in the custody of an iron hand from which we cannot escape. That, I thnk, is the significance of the strangely violent figure used by the Prophet Isaiah: "The Lord said unto me with a strong hand." The divine calling laid hold of the young prophet as though with a "strong hand" that imprisoned him like a vice! He felt he had no alternative! He was carried along by divine coercion! "Necessity was laid" upon him! He was "in bonds" and he must obey... And so it is that the manner of one man's "call" may be very different for the manner of another man's "call," but in the essential matter, they are one and the same.[235]

GROWING IN KNOWLEDGE, LIVING BY FAITH

UNIT 12

REVIEW

(1) What should a believer do before saying "Yes" to God's call? _____

(2) What are the basic instructions for discerning God's will? _____

(3) What are possible consequences for disobeying God's call? _____

(4) Based on Jonah's experience (Jonah 1:3-17), who pays the cost for a believer's rebellion? _____

(5) Is it your honest intent to know and do the will of God? _____ Why is this foundationally important? _____

NEGLECT NOT: SERVICE

Neglect not the gift that is in you [stop neglecting; don't be careless] but stir it up to full flame.
—1 Timothy 4:14

Timothy's timidity hindered the use of his gift (pastor/teacher), and Paul admonished him to "get over it." The point is clear: believers are not to allow fear, cowardice, timidity, influence of others, money, business, or any other thing to prevent fulfillment of God's call to vocational ministry. It's always disappointing and grievous to see someone quit who is gifted for the specific call to vocational ministry.

The word "gift" in this text refers to the multiplicity of spiritual gifts Paul cites in 1 Corinthians 12, Romans 12, and Ephesians 4. Believers (not just those called to vocational ministry like Timothy) have at least one gift to use in service to Christ. It may be the gift of administration, teaching, exhortation, hospitality, helps, or music and singing. You will only be truly fulfilled when you discover your gift(s) and offer yourself that way for Christian service.

Wise use of gift(s) enlarges the opportunity to impact others. It fulfills the design of God for your life, benefits the church, and glorifies God. You should work daily to develop and sharpen your gift(s) for the greatest possible usefulness. Grow your giftedness through study, prayer, and utilization.

UNDERSTANDING GOD'S WILL
UNIT 12

REFLECT—*Consider What This Means*

(1) What insights do you gain from the following passages regarding godly counsel?
   Proverbs 11:14 _____
   Proverbs 15:22 _____
   Acts 13:5 _____
(2) Are you willing to do the will of God whatever that may be? Obedience to what you hear from God is imperative for further revelations.
(3) How might hypocrisy affect your ability to hear God's direction? _____
_____
_____

(4) List what you count as the gifts God has bestowed upon your life. _____
_____

What do they potentially reveal about God's call to you? _____
(5) List the spiritual markers of your life in sequence, and see how God may or may not be guiding to vocational ministry. _____
_____
_____

Do these markers seem to confirm God's call to ministry? Why or why not?
_____
_____

(6) What does Acts 16:6-10 indicate about the Holy Spirit's leadership? _____
_____

Have you ever experienced the divine impression of the Spirit to say, do, or avoid something or someone? To change plans? If so, describe it. _____
_____
_____
_____

(7) How might a period of tribulation in your life bring special challenges to knowing God's will?
_____
_____
_____

GROWING IN KNOWLEDGE, LIVING BY FAITH

UNIT 12

RESPOND—*What Will You Do with What You Know?*

(1) Note the specifics of David's request in Psalm 25:4-5: "show me, teach me, lead me." Prayer of this substance and intensity will not go unanswered. Using this prayer as a model, frame your own prayer to God in quest of His will.

- Show me: _____
  _____
  _____
  _____
  _____

- Teach me: _____
  _____
  _____
  _____
  _____

- Lead me: _____
  _____
  _____
  _____
  _____
  _____

(2) Has God called you? If so, embrace it with all your being! Say, "Lord here am I; send me, send me." Once the call is clarified, you need to press forward in faith. There will be things you don't know about the future and all that will be required, but trust God a step at a time. As with a scroll, God may unroll a bit at a time to reveal His awesome plan for your life—so wait patiently and walk in the light you are given.

(3) Look up Psalm 18:28, and apply it to a divine call to ministry. _____
_____
_____
_____

(4) Psalm 32:8 has meant much to me in my ministry. What promise does it indicate, and what can you do with that in your own life? _____
_____
_____

(5) Have you been neglecting to put your spiritual giftedness to work? If so, stop neglecting the use of your gift(s) in Kingdom service. Change your ways, and start using your gifts—*now!*

GROWING IN KNOWLEDGE, LIVING BY FAITH

ENDNOTES

1 G. Campbell Morgan, *The Westminster Pulpit* (Westwood, NJ: Fleming H. Revell, 1954), 305-306.

INTRODUCTION
2 Oswald Chambers, *My Utmost for His Highest* (Grand Rapids: Discovery House, 1992), May 10.
3 C.H. Spurgeon, *The Sword and the Trowel*, September, 1884.
4 Marie A. Barnett, "Breathe – This is the Air I Breathe" (Mercy / Vineyard Publishing, 1995).
5 In John Harder, Ed., *The Evangelist* (Edmonton, Alberta: Evangelical Tract Distributors, 2011), 2.

UNIT 1–BELIEVE THIS!
6 C.H. Spurgeon, *The Early Years: C.H. Spurgeons' Autobiography* (London: Banner of Truth, 1962), 167.
7 John Stott, *The Message of Galatians* (London and Downers Grove: IVP, 1968), 24.
8 From A.W. Pink, *The Attributes of God* (Grand Rapids: Baker, 1991), Chapter 9.
9 Norman Geisler, *Systematic Theology*, Vol 2 (Minneapolis: Bethany House, 2003), 279.
10 C.H. Spurgeon, *Morning and Evening* (Great Britain: Christian Focus Publications, 1994), July 12.
11 W.A. Criswell, *The Criswell Study Bible* (Nashville: Nelson Publishing Company, 1979), 1459.
12 Charles C. Ryrie, *The Ryrie Study Bible* (Chicago: Moody Press, 1994), 1991.
13 John Stott, "Teacher and Lord," (Minneapolis: *Decision Magazine*, March 1961).
14 W.A. Criswell, *Why I Preach that the Bible is Literally True* (Nashville: Broadman Press, 1969), 19-20.
15 In Shelton Smith, Ed., *Great Preaching on Christ*, Vol. 19 (Murfreesboro: Sword of the Lord Publishers, 2002), 178.
16 John Stott, *You Can Trust The Bible*, (Grand Rapids: Discovery House, 1991), 69.
17 C.H. Spurgeon, "Particular Redemption" (*Metropolitan Tabernacle Pulpit*. Pasadena, Texas: Pilgrim Publications, 1976), February 28, 1858.
18 Adrian Rogers, *You Can Be Sure*, (Love Worth Finding Radio Broadcast), Program 2063.
19 John MacArthur, *MacArthur Study Bible* (Nashville: Thomas Nelson, 1997), I Peter 1:5.
20 In Norman Geisler, *Systematic Theology*, Vol. 3 (Minneapolis: Bethany House, 2004), 309.
21 John MacArthur, *The MacArthur Study Bible* (electronic ed.) Nashville: Word Pub. 1997), Gal. 5:16.
22 J. I. Packer, *Concise Theology: A Guide to Historic Christian Beliefs* (Wheaton: Crossway Books, 1994), 180.
23 Stott, *Baptism and Fullness* (London: IVP, 1975), 45.
24 Leonard Ravenhill, *Why Revival Tarries* (Grand Rapids: Bethany House Publishers, 2004), 54.
25 C.H. Spurgeon, "The Holy Ghost – The Great Teacher" (*Metropolitan Tabernacle Pulpit*. Pasadena, Texas: Pilgrim Publications, 1976), November 18, 1855.
26 Stott, *Baptism and Fullness*, 60.
27 In Curtis Hutson, Ed. *Great Preaching on the Second Coming* (Murfreesboro: Sword of the Lord Publishers, 1989), 109.
28 Paul E. Little, *Know What You Believe* (Wheaton: Victor Books, 1979), 189.
29 Spurgeon, *Morning and Evening*, April 20.
30 In Smith, *Great Preaching on Christ*, 175.
31 John MacArthur, *Truth Matters* (Nashville: Nelson Publishers, 2004), 71.
32 John Stott, *The Bible and the Crisis of Authority* (London: Falcon, 1972), 14.

UNIT 2–THE NEW BIRTH
33 D.L. Moody, *The Way to God and How to Find It* (Cosmos Classics, 2005), 23.
34 Louisa Fletcher, *The Land of Beginning Again* (Boston: Small, Maynard and Company Publishers, 1921), 3.
35 Spurgeon, *Morning and Evening*, March 6.
36 John Piper, "The Agonizing Problem of the Assurance of Salvation" (www.desiringgod.org), accessed September 13, 2010).
37 Ibid.
38 John R. Rice, *Rice Reference Bible*, (Nashville: Nelson Publishing, 1981), xii.
39 Ibid., xiii.
40 D.L. Moody, *Prevailing Prayer: What Hinders It* (Chicago: F.H. Revell Company, 1884), 68.
41 Horatius Bonar, "I lay my Sins on Jesus" (Songs for the Wilderness, 1843), www.cyberhymnal.org., accessed October 15, 2010.
42 David Beatty, "It's Different Now" (artists.letssingit.com/skeeter-davis-lyrics-its-different-now., accessed October 15, 2010).
43 Vance Havner, *Messages on Revival* (Grand Rapids: Baker Book House, 1958), 117-118.
44 C.H. Spurgeon, *Spurgeon's Sermons, Vol. 2* (Grand Rapids: Baker Books, 1999), 309.
45 Adrian Rogers, *Adrianisms* (Memphis: Love Worth Finding Ministries, 2006), 156.
46 H.F. Stevenson, Ed. *God's Man: Studies in 2 Timothy* (The Keswick Week 1969. London: Marshall, Morgan, and Scott, 1969), 51.

UNIT 3–THE SIGNIFICANCE OF THE BIBLE
47 Donald S. Whitney, *Spiritual Disciplines of the Christian Life: Ten Questions to Diagnose Your Spiritual Health* (Colorado Springs: NavPress, 2002), 26.

48 A.W. Pink, *Studies in the Scriptures*, Vol. 5 (Sovereign Grace Publishers, Inc. (September 28, 2001), 230.
49 In A.T. Pierson, *George Mueller of Bristol* (Grand Rapids: Fleming Revell Company, 1899).
50 "Archaeology and the Bible" (Christiananswers.net/archaeology), accessed December 27, 2010.
51 Ibid.
52 Ibid.
53 Ibid.
54 "Facing the Challenge" (www.facingthechallenge.org), accessed December 22, 2010.
55 Waine-Ann McLaughlin, "How Archaeology Proves the Bible," *Prevail Magazine* (www.prevailmagazine.org) accessed December 27, 2010.
56 W.A. Criswell, *My Favorite Text* (Criswell Sermon Library. December 12, 1975), www.wacriswell.org, accessed August 2, 2010)
57 John MacArthur, *Why Believe the Bible* (Ventura, CA: Regal, 2007), 36.
58 D.L. Moody, *Pleasures and Profit in Bible Study* (Grand Rapids: Fleming Revell Publishers, 1895), 51.
59 John W. Stott, *Culture and the Bible* (Downers Grove: IVP, 1981), 33.
60 Whitney, 61.
61 John MacArthur, *A Faith To Grow On* (Nashville: Thomas Nelson, 2000), 74.
62 Max Lucado, *Life Lessons – Book of Psalms* (Lubbock, Texas: Word Publishing, 1997), 6.
63 Graeme Goldsworthy, *According to Plan* (Nottingham, England: Intervarsity Press, 1991).
64 In Moody, *Pleasures and Profit of Bible Study*, 79.
65 C.H. Spurgeon, "How to Read the Bible" (Sermon # 1503, 1879), *Metropolitan Tabernacle Pulpit*. (Pasadena, Texas: Pilgrim Publications, 1976).
66 John Stott, *The Contemporary Christian* (Downers Grove: Intervarsity Press, 1995), 104.
67 D.L. Moody, *The D.L. Moody Book: A Living Message from the Words of D.L. Moody* (New York: Fleming H. Revell, 1900), 223.
68 John Stott, *The Letters of John: Tyndale New Testament Commentaries* (Grand Rapids: Eerdmans, 1988), 119.
69 C.H. Spurgeon, "How to Read the Bible."

UNIT 4–OVERVIEW OF THE BIBLE
70 John Stott, *The Message of 2 Timothy* (London and Downers Grove: IVP, 1973), 102.
71 In Criswell, *The Criswell Study Bible*, xvii.
72 Philip Comfort and Walter Elwell. *The Tyndale Bible Dictionary* (Carol Stream: Tyndale House Publishers, 2001), 172.
73 B.B. Warfield, *The Formation of the Canon of the New Testament* (Philadelphia: American Sunday Union, 1982).
74 Moody, *Pleasures and Profit in Bible Study*, 32-33.
75 John Stott, *The Preacher's Portrait* (London: Tyndale Press, 1961), 100.
76 W.A. Criswell, "My Favorite Text" (Criswell Sermon Library, December 12, 1975), www.wacriswell.org, accessed August 2, 2010.
77 C.H. Spurgeon, "Sin: It's Spring-Head, Stream and Sea" (*Metropolitan Tabernacle Pulpit*. Pasadena: Pilgrim Publications, 1976), May 10, 1891.
78 In Marshall D. Johnson, *The Evolution of Christianity: Twelve Crises that Shaped the Church* (Continuum International Publishing Group, 2005).
79 Francis Dixon, *What Every Christian Should Know* (Bournemouth, England: Landsdowne Bible School and Postal Fellowship, 1964), June 9.
80 John MacArthur, *How to Meet the Enemy* (Wheaton: Victory Books, 1992), 111.

UNIT 5–PRAYER, FASTING, AND SOLITUDE
81 C.H. Spurgeon, *A Puritan Catechism. What is Sanctification?* (The Spurgeon Archive, www.spurgeon.org/catechis.htm), accessed September 14, 2010.
82 Ray C. Stedman, *If God Be For Us, Sermon* (Palo Alto, California: Discovery House Publishing, 1976).
83 Dietrich Bonhoeffer, *Life Together and Prayer Book of the Bible* (Dietrich Bonhoeffer Works, Vol. 5) (Minneapolis: Fortress Press, 2005), 146.
84 In Ray Comfort, Ed., *The Evidence Bible* (Gainesville, Florida: Bridge-Logos Publishers, 2002), 634.
85 Matthew Henry and Philip Henry, *The Miscellaneous Works of the Rev. Matthew Henry* (Robinson, 1833), 433.
86 In E.M. Bounds, *Power Through Prayer* (Racine, Wisconsin: Treasures Media, Inc., undated), 16.
87 A.W. Tozer, *The Divine Conquest* (Harrisburg, Pennsylvania: Christian Publications Inc., 1950), 22.
88 E.M. Bounds, *Power Through Prayer*, (New York: Cosimo, Inc., 2009), 121.
89 In Moody, *Pleasures and Profit in Bible Study*, 94.
90 John Bisagno, *The Power of Positive Praying* (Grand Rapids: Zondervan, 1972), 10.
91 In Larry J. Michael, *Spurgeon on Leadership* (Grand Rapids: Kregel Publications, 2003), 71.
92 Jon Courson, *Courson's Application Commentary* (Nashville: Nelson Publishing Company, 2004), Matthew 6: 9 -13.

ENDNOTES

93 In E.M. Bounds, *Purpose in Prayer* (Grand Rapids: Fleming H. Revell Company, 1920), 71.
94 Andrew Murray, *With Christ in the School of Prayer* (New Kensington, Pennsylvania: Whitaker House, 1981), 34.
95 Courson, Matthew 6: 14-15.
96 Jean Calvin, John Calvin, A.W. Morrison, David W. Torrance, Thomas F. Torrance, Thomas H. Louis Parker, *A Harmony of the Gospels*, Matthew, Mark, and Luke (Grand Rapids: Wm. B. Eerdmans Publishing, 1995), 213.
97 Matthew Henry, *Matthew Henry Commentary on the Whole Bible, Vol. 3* (Peabody: Hendrickson Publishers, 1991), 255.
98 Thomas Ken, "Awake My Soul, and with the Sun," *Thomas Ken, Manual of Prayers for the Use of the Scholars of Winchester College, 1674*, www.cyberhymnal.org/htm/a/w/awakemys.htm, accessed January 8, 2011.
99 D.A. Carson, *A Call to Spiritual Reformation* (Grand Rapids: Baker Book House, 1992).
100 Oswald Chambers, *My Utmost for His Highest*, June 20.
101 Spurgeon, *Morning and Evening*, February 6.
102 In J. Harold Smith, *Fast Your Way to Health* (Thomas Nelson Publishers: Nashville, 1979), 89.
103 In Whitney, 164.
104 Bill Bright, *Your Personal Guide to Fasting and Prayer* (Orlando: New Life Publications, 1997).
105 Michael D. Warden, *The Transformed Heart* (Austin, Texas: Ascent Books and Media, 2008), 80.
106 Spurgeon, *Morning and Evening*, October 12.
107 Warden, 85.
108 Andrew Murray, *Waiting on God* (New Kensington: Whitaker House, 1983), 108-109.
109 In Warren Wiersbe, *The Best of A.W. Tozer* (Grand Rapids: Baker Book House, 1978), 151-152.
110 C.H. Spurgeon, "Solitude, Silence and Submission, Sermon" (*Metropolitan Tabernacle Pulpit*. Pasadena: Pilgrim Publications, 1976) June 13, 1886.
111 J.C. Ryle, *Holiness* (La Vergne: Lightning Source, 2001), 22.
112 Martin Lloyd Jones, *Preachers and Preaching, Vol. 2* (Grand Rapids: Zondervan, 1972), 171.
113 John Bunyan, *The Complete Works* (Bradley, Garreteon, 1873), 80.
114 In Bounds, *Purpose in Prayer*, 21.
115 Spurgeon, *Sermons of Rev. C.H. Spurgeon of London*, 21.
116 David Jeremiah, *Prayer the Great Adventure* (The Doubleday Religious Publishing Group, 1999),58.
117 Corrie Ten Boone, *Each New Day* (Minneapolis: World Wide Publications, 1978), October 16.
118 C.J. Mahaney, *Humility: True Greatness* (New York: Multnomah Publishing, 2005), 79.
119 Bounds, *Power Through Prayer*, 19.
120 J. Wilbur Chapman, *And Peter* (Grand Rapids: Fleming H. Revell Company, 1896), 108.
121 John Bisagno, *Positive Praying*, Preface.

UNIT 6–BAPTISM
122 J.I. Packer, *Growing in Christ* (Wheaton: Crossway Books, 1994), 144.
123 C.H. Spurgeon, "The Dying Thief in a New Light, Sermon" (*Metropolitan Tabernacle Pulpit*. Pasadena: Pilgrim Publications, 1976), August 23, 1885.
124 Warren Wiersbe, *Wiersbe's Expository Commentary on the New Testament, John 3: 6-7* (Wheaton: SP Publications, 1992).
125 Spurgeon, *Morning and Evening*, September 11.

UNIT 7–THE LORD'S SUPPER
126 Courson, 1 Corinthians 11: 23–26.
127 Curtis Hutson and John Reynolds, ED., *Soul Stirring Songs and Hymns*. (Murfreesboro: Tennessee, 1989), 243.
128 John MacArthur, *The MacArthur Study Bible, 1 Corinthians 11:27* (Nashville: Nelson Publishers, 2004).
129 Ravenhill, 54.
130 Charles A. Tindley, "Nothing Between" (www.hymnsite.com, accessed October 15, 2010), #373.

UNIT 8–STEWARDSHIP
131 David McKinley, *The Life You Were Born to Give: Why It's Better to Live than to Receive* (Nashville: W Publishing Group, 2006), 119.
132 Courson, 2 Corinthians 8:5.
133 In Harold Myra, Lawrence and Marshall Shelley, *The Leadership Secrets of Billy Graham* (Grand Rapids: Zondervan, 2005), 107.
134 Spurgeon, "A Best Donation", (*Metropolitan Tabernacle Pulpit*, April 5, 1891).
135 Gordon MacDonald and Art Farstad. *Believer's Bible Commentary: Old and New Testaments, 2 Corinthians 8:9* (Nashville: Thomas Nelson, 1995)
136 MacArthur, *The MacArthur Study Bible*, 2 Corinthians 8:9.
137 Hutson and Reynolds, 5.
138 John Bunyan, *Pilgrim's Progress* (New York: P. F. Collier and Son, 1909), 271.

GROWING IN KNOWLEDGE, LIVING BY FAITH

ENDNOTES

139 John W. Weddel, *Your Study Bible* (Philadelphia: The Sunday School Times Company, 1918), 131.
140 In Charles Spurgeon Quotes (christian-quotes.ochristian.com, accessed September 16, 2010), 13.
141 Richard J. Foster, *Celebration of Discipline* (New York: Harper Collins, 1998), 190.
142 Donald S. Whitney, *Spiritual Disciples of the Christian Life* (Colorado Springs: Nav Press, 19910, 147.
143 "More Than 54,000 Great Quotations To Inspire You!" Cybernation.com, accessed January 8, 2011.
144 In Stephen Tomkins, *John Wesley: A Biography* (Grand Rapids: Eerdmans Publishing, 2003), 157.
145 In Whitney, 150.
146 At Discipleshiptools.org, accessed September 15, 2010.
147 Billy Graham, *Rules for Christian Living* (Charlotte: Billy Graham Evangelistic Association, 1953), 40.
148 Kent Hughes, "Grace of Giving", Sermon (PreachingTodaySermons.com).
149 Spurgeon, "A Cheerful Giver is Beloved of God", Sermon # 835, (*Metropolitan Tabernacle Pulpit*, August 27, 1868).
150 Whitney, 139.
151 C.S. Lewis, *The Complete C.S. Lewis Signature Classics* (New York: HarperCollins Publishers, 2002), 52.
152 Matthew Henry, *Henry Commentary on the Whole Bible*, Luke 6:38.
153 Ray Boltz, "Thank You" (Gaither MusicASCAP, 1988), www.lyricstime.com., accessed October 15, 2010.

UNIT 9–SATAN
154 W.A. Criswell, "Satan", March 16, 1958 (The W.A. Criswell Sermon Library, wacriswell.com).
155 Jack R. Taylor, *Victory over the Devil* (Nashville: Broadman Press, 1973), 9.
156 In ThinkExist.com, "Satan Quotes and Quotations" (accessed September 15, 2010).
157 Jerry Rankin, *Spiritual Warfare: The Battle for God's Glory* Nashville: B&H Publishing Group, 2009), 20.
158 Thomas a' Kempis, *Imitation of Christ* (Peabody: Hendrickson Publishers, 2004).
159 At ThinkExist.com, accessed September 15, 2010.
160 John MacArthur, *Why Believe the Bible*, 143-144.
161 Courson, Matthew 6:13.
162 Martyn Lloyd-Jones, *The Christian Soldier* (Grand Rapids: Baker, 1977), 179.
163 In Jack Taylor, *Victory Over the Devil* (Nashville: Broadman Press, 1973), Foreword.
164 M. R. Vincent, *Word Studies in the New Testament* (1 John 2:18) (Bellingham, WA: Logos Research Systems, Inc., 2002).
165 Courson, 1 John 4: 3.
166 In "Coming of Christ Sermon Illustrations". moreillustrations.com/Illustrations/coming, accessed January 8, 2011.
167 In Curtis Hutson, Ed., *Great Preaching on Judgment* (Murfreesboro: Sword of the Lord Publishers, 1990), 109.

UNIT 10–WITNESSING
168 Bailey Smith, *Real Evangelism* (Nashville: Broadman Press, 1978), 163-164.
169 Ibid., 118.
170 In C. E. Autrey, *You Can Win Souls* (Nashville: Broadman Press, 1961), 6.
171 In Adrian Rogers, *Adrianisms*, 174.
172 In Curtis Hutson, *Great Preaching on Soulwinning* (Murfreesboro: Sword of the Lord Publishers, 1989), 234.
173 John MacArthur, *The MacArthur Study Bible* (electronic ed.) Nashville: Word Pub. 1997), Gal. 5:16.
174 In Bill Swainson, *Encarta Book of Quotations* (New York: Macmillan, 2000), 422.
175 Oswald J. Sanders, *The Revival We Need* (New York: The Christian Alliance Publishing Company,1925), Chapter 3.
176 John MacArthur, "Beware of the Pretenders: The Eternal Security of the Christian," Sermon (biblebb.com, accessed February 10, 2011).
177 C. H. Spurgeon, *The Soul Winner* (New Kensington, Pennsylvania: Whitaker House, 1995), 172-173.
178 Alexander Alonzo Phelps. *Purity and Power* (Boston: Advent Christian Publication Society, 1905), 195.
179 C. H.Spurgeon, *Spurgeon's Sermons on Soulwinning* (Grand Rapids: Kregel Publications, 1995), 33.
180 Adrian Rogers. "Who are the Elect?" (Youtube. Accessed Sept 5, 2010).
181 Adrian Rogers, *The Passion of Christ and the Purpose of Life* (Wheaton: Crossway Books, 2005), 67.
182 Lee Weeks, Doctrine of election too transcendent for human explanation, Patterson says (Baptist Press: September 1, 1998).
183 Spurgeon, *Morning and Evening*, February 1.
184 C. H. Spurgeon, "Kept From Iniquity" (*Metropolitan Tabernacle Pulpit*, September 29, 1895).
185 In Paul S. Rees, *Stir up the Gift* (Grand Rapids: Zondervan, 1952), 106.

UNIT 11–CHURCH
186 At Servant's Heart Fellowship (servantheartfellowship.com, accessed September 15, 2010).
187 In Lewis A. Drummond, *The Evangelist* (Lubbock, Texas: Word Publishing, 2001), 172.
188 In James D. Simmons. *Milton Studies 18* (Pittsburgh, Pennsylvania: University of Pittsburgh Press, 1990), 7.
189 Spurgeon, "Joining a Church" (*Metropolitan Tabernacle Pulpit*, Sermon # 3411).

190 In Ray Comfort, Ed., *The Evidence Bible* (Gainesville, Florida: Bridge-Logos Publishers, 2002), 456.
191 Jerry Bridges, *I Give You Glory, O God* (Waterville, Maine: Thorndike Press, 2002), 16.
192 *Church Administration*, July 1992. (c) 1992, The Sunday School Board of the SBC. www.founders.org/journal, accessed January 8, 2011.
193 W.W. Wiersbe, *The Bible Exposition Commentary, Php 3:13* (Wheaton Illinois: Victor Books, 1996).
194 Spurgeon, *Morning and Evening*, March 2.
195 Lewis Drummond, *The Canvas Cathedral* (Nashville, TN: W Publication Group, 2001), 65-66.
196 Drummond, *The Canvas Cathedral*, 65–66.
197 At ThinkExist.com, accessed February 10, 2011.
198 W.A. Criswell, "St. Patrick Was a Baptist Preacher" Sermon, March 16, 1958, (The W.A. Criswell Sermon Library. wacriswell.com, accessed February 10, 2011).
199 John MacArthur, "Qualified Servants for the Church—Deacons, Part 1"(1 Timothy 3:8-13, Tape GC 54-25).
200 Connie Snow, *Wit from Adrian Rogers*, (Taken from Sermon Notes of Connie Snow March, 1973-February, 2005), www.artfulaskers.com/page/page/4718398.htm. Accessed August 2, 2010.
201 William Barclay, *The New Daily Study Bible* (Louisville, Kentucky: Westminster John Knox Press, 2002), 171.
202 *Expository Dictionary of Bible Words* (Grand Rapids: Zondervan, 1985), 60-62.
203 Spurgeon, *The Ascension of Christ*.
204 In Bill Adler, *Ask Billy Graham* (Nashville: Thomas Nelson, 2007), 43.
205 Faris Whitsell, *Basic Evangelism* (Grand Rapids: Zondervan, 1949), 117.
206 Wayne Barber, "Ephesians 4:11-13: Preserving the Unity of the Spirit, Part 3" (preceptaustin.com, accessed February 10, 2011).
207 In John Scott Trent, *Evangelists in Action* (Orlando: Daniels Publishers, 1971), 14.
208 Whitsell, 123.
209 Robert E. Coleman, *The Master Plan of Evangelism* (Old Tappan, New Jersey: Fleming H. Revell Company, 1988), 123-124.
210 Ibid., 119-120.
211 In J. D. Douglas, Ed. *The Work of the Evangelist* (Minneapolis: World Wide Publishers, 1984), 171.
212 C.E. Matthews, *The Southern Baptist Program of Evangelism* (Nashville: Convention Press, 1956), 92-93.
213 Ibid., 95.
214 Billy Graham, John 3:16, Sermon.

UNIT 12–UNDERSTANDING GOD'S WILL
215 William Booth, "Duty", A Letter sent to fellow comrades from William Booth (Barnabas Ministries UK, July 20, 2009, ernestanderson.wordpress.com, accessed September 15, 2010).
216 *The South in the Building of the Nation* (Southern Historical Publication Society, 1909), 131.
217 In Roy B. Zuck, *The Speaker's Quote Book* (Grand Rapids: Kregel Publications, 1997), 169.
218 Spurgeon, *Morning and Evening*, September 10.
219 In B. Patterson and D.L. Goetz, *Deepening Your Conversation with God*,Vol.7 (Minneapolis.: Bethany House Publishers, 1999), 148.
220 In Missions slogans and notables quotes from missionaries(www.project1615.org/quotes.htm., accessed October 15, 2010).
221 D. L. Moody (vsb.gospel.com).
222 Max Lucado & T.A. Gibbs *Grace for the Moment: Inspirational Thoughts for Each Day of the Year* (Nashville: J. Countryman, 2000), 218.
223 Paul Little, *Affirming the Will of God* (Downers Grove: InterVarsity Press, 1999), 9.
224 In Dan Hayes, "Motivating Reasons to Pray" (www.startingwithgod.com), accessed January 8,2008.
225 Richard Allen Bodey, *Inside the Sermon* (Grand Rapids: Baker Book House, 1990), 125-126.
226 C.H. Spurgeon, *Lectures to My Students* (Grand Rapids: Zondervan, 1970), 30.
227 In Harder, 6.
228 Henry Blackaby, *Experiencing God*, (Nashville: Broadman and Holman, 2008), 194.
229 A. W. Pink, "The Leading of the Holy Spirit" (1934, www.johnbunyan.org/PDFs/loth.pdf., accessed July 25, 2010).
230 C. H. Spurgeon, (1993). *Psalms*. Crossway Classic Commentaries (Wheaton, Illinois: Crossway Books), 126.
231 Jim Elliot Quote. www.wheaton.edu/bgc/archives. (October 28, 1949 entry) 174. Accessed January 8, 2011.
232 Amanda Smith, *An Autobiography of Mrs. Amanda Smith* (Chicago: Myer & Brother Publisher, 1893), 246.
233 F.E. Marsh, *1,000 Bible Study Outlines* (Grand Rapids: Kregel Publications, 1970), 30.
234 In Curtis Hutson and John Reynolds, Ed., *Soul Stirring Songs & Hymns* (Murfreesboro, Tennessee: Sword of the Lord Publishers, 1989), 331.
235 J. H. Jowett, *The Preacher: His Life and Work* (New York: George H. Doran Company, 1912), 16-17.